The Yale Edition of the Works of St. Thomas More

SELECTED WORKS

*Published by the St. Thomas More Project,
Yale University, under the auspices of
Gerard L. Carroll and Joseph B. Murray,
Trustees of the Michael P. Grace, II, Trust,
and with the support of the National Endowment
for the Humanities*

King Richard III (National Portrait Gallery)

ST. THOMAS MORE

The History of King Richard III and Selections from the English and Latin Poems

edited by

RICHARD S. SYLVESTER

NEW HAVEN AND LONDON, YALE UNIVERSITY PRESS
1976

Designed by Sally Sullivan
and set in Baskerville type.
Printed in the United States of America by
Vail-Ballou Press, Binghamton, N.Y.

Published in Great Britain, Europe, and Africa by
Yale University Press, Ltd., London.
Distributed in Latin America by Kaiman & Polon,
Inc., New York City; in Australasia by Book & Film
Services, Artarmon, N.S.W., Australia; in Japan by
John Weatherhill, Inc., Tokyo.

FOREWORD

The present volume is the third to appear in the modernized series of selected works of St. Thomas More, a series designed to make available to the general reader works which have already appeared or are about to appear in the Yale Edition of the Complete Works. Companion volumes published earlier are *Selected Letters,* ed. E. F. Rogers (1961), and *Utopia,* ed. E. Surtz (1964). In preparing *Richard III and Selections from the English and Latin Poems,* I have had the assistance, always reliable and helpful, at times approaching devotion, of Mary Alice Hardy and Helen Whall-Seligman. Without their aid, for which I am deeply grateful, this "Richardus minor" would have seen the light at a much later date. The Thomas More Project at Yale has been blessed over the years with an excellent staff of research assistants and graduate students. To them this volume is dedicated—*quoniam ab his herbis quibus literis coeperunt euirescere, egregiam aliquando frugem spero.*

Richard S. Sylvester
Executive Editor

CONTENTS

CONTENTS   ix

INTRODUCTION

The history of Thomas More's *History of King Richard III*
must begin with a brief summary of the complicated processes
through which that text has been transmitted to us.[1] One should
not, first of all, speak of a "text," but rather of "texts." More
wrote his *History*, to use the words of his nephew, William
Rastell, "about the yeare of our Lorde .1513."; but when he
wrote it he did so in both English and Latin, producing in fact,
two separate but intimately related narratives, the one, in the
vernacular, for a native audience, the other, the *Historia
Richardi Tertius*, in the international language of Europe. Both
versions of the narrative were left unfinished and neither was
published during More's lifetime.[2] It is clear, however, that
manuscript copies of at least the English text[3] were known in the
1530s and it was from some such text, garbled and corrupted in
many details, that the *History* first appeared in print in Richard

1. For a full survey of the textual problems involved in the study of
the *Richard*, see my discussion in Volume 2 of the *Yale Edition of the
Complete Works of St. Thomas More* (New Haven, 1963), cited hereafter as *CW 2*. The Bibliography that follows this Introduction provides a selective list for further reading and takes note of recent work
(to 1975) that has been concerned with More's work and with
Richard's reign.

2. For the English text printed here, based on that published by
Rastell in his 1557 edition of More's *English Works*, see below, A Note
on the Text. For the relationship between the English and Latin versions of the *History*, see *CW 2*, liv–lix. More's *Utopia* (1516) was
written only in Latin.

3. An early draft of the Latin version is preserved at the College of
Arms (MS. Arundel 43) but there is no evidence that it circulated
widely.

Grafton's edition of *The Chronicle of John Harding* in 1543. In 1548, and again in 1550, a slightly better version was included in Grafton's editions of Edward Hall's *Chronicle*. All of these early issues were severely castigated by Rastell when, in 1557, he published the English *History* from a holograph manuscript. Rastell's text thus became the basis for later printings of More's narrative in the chronicles of the Elizabethan period.[4]

The portrait More gives us of the last Yorkist king has occasioned no end of discussion. Although many of the crimes with which his Richard is charged will probably, given the extant evidence, never be proven, so powerful is the dramatic language of More's narrative that the conventional view of Richard III in English history is essentially his. It was More who first gave real literary shape and form to the host of rumors and covert tales that circulated through the court of Henry VII after Richard's death at Bosworth Field in 1485. And it was More's narrative, whether read in the *English Works* of 1557 or in the histories of Grafton, Hall, and Holinshed, that provided Shakespeare with both plot and inspiration for his *Tragedy of Richard III*. Modern historical scholarship questions many details of this "standard" version; it points to the accomplishments of Richard's short reign (July 1483–August 1485), singling out especially his efforts at administrative reform. Yet the early accusations linger, like unexorcisable demons, around the figure of the tormented king. Richard may not have slain Henry VI with his own hands, he may not have helped convey the Duke of Clarence to his miserable death (even More, it will be noted, doubts the legend on these points), but there remains the matter of the summary executions of the Queen's relatives and of Lord Hastings, deaths which could not have occurred without Richard's consent. Above all, the little princes, the Duke of York and the Prince of Wales, Richard's nephews: they were last seen alive in the opening months of Richard's reign. No explanation

---

4. For a good survey of the chronicle tradition, see F. J. Levy, *Tudor Historical Thought* (San Marino, Calif., 1967). The Latin *Historia* was first published at Louvain in 1565.

for their disappearance was ever offered by the king and, until evidence comes to light that would fix the burden of their deaths on another, More's charge, which was the charge of his age, must remain on the record.

It is easy enough, on the other hand, for those who would discover justifiable dignity and not tyrannous dishonor in Richard III, to point to many errors of fact in More's narrative. He will often get names wrong and he will often embroider details. In the past, Richard's supporters have doubted that More actually wrote the *History*, finding its gruesome features beneath the dignity of an author who was later to become a legend himself—for the integrity of his life and death. As early as the late sixteenth century and as recently as the early twentieth, the authorship of the narrative has been assigned[5] to John Cardinal Morton (1420–1500), in whose household More had been raised and who was himself a key figure in the deposing of Richard before he became, as Archbishop of Canterbury and Lord Chancellor, the chief administrator of Henry VII. But More's claim to the *History*, as recent scholarship has firmly established,[6] cannot be denied. For better or worse, the character, and the conscience, of the king as we have come to know him are those given him by Thomas More.

With the question of authorship settled, other speculations soon arise. If More did indeed write the *History*, why did he do it? What could he have hoped to accomplish by setting down such a story and, moving the inquiry a step farther, why, once he had undertaken the task, did he leave his work both unfinished and unpublished? Several points need to be made, as one attempts to suggest the lines upon which answers to these quite legitimate queries might be developed. First of all, More did not, most assuredly, originate the terrible stories about Richard III. Before 1513, other writers—men with official or

5. By Sir John Harington in his *Metamorphosis of Ajax* (1596), and by the *Dictionary of National Biography* and the *Cambridge History of English Literature*.

6. The evidence is summarized in *CW 2*, lix–lxiii.

semiofficial positions at the court of Henry VII[7]—had already set down most of the horrific details. Whether or not More read these accounts, he grew to maturity among men (Morton among them) who had lived through the events of Richard's reign and who could, if they would, furnish him with many an anecdote. In the *History,* More often seems to rely on oral testimony of this kind. Phrases like "it is for truth reported," "this have I by credible information learned," "wise men say," etc., abound as his tale develops. We may doubt the truth of what is being said, but it is difficult not to believe that, as More says, men were indeed saying things like this. Often, too, the narrative, for all its hearsay (if vividly colloquial) qualities, proves to be correct when its statements are checked against the extant documentary evidence.[8] The recorder of London, as More says, had just been appointed to his position when he was asked to second Buckingham's speech to the London citizens; Ralph Shaa (More calls him "John") did die not long after his "shameful" sermon in support of Richard; the men (John Green, William Slaughter, Miles Forest, John Dighton) whom More names as directly involved in the murder of the princes can at least be shown to have been associated with the Yorkist court.

More lived and wrote in an atmosphere which found little that was good in the character of King Richard. Yet it must be emphasized that his account cannot be viewed as simply another piece of government propaganda designed to strengthen the somewhat shaky claim of Henry VII to the throne. More never showed himself to be anti-Yorkist and he was, in fact, quite critical of many of Henry VII's policies, as he was to be, twenty years later, of Henry VIII's. In 1509, he could rejoice at the

7. Pietro Carmeliano (d. 1527) and Bernard André (d. 1522), both court poets, are examples. For their written accounts, and those of others, see *CW 2,* lxx–lxxx.

8. The narrative of Dominic Mancini (see Bibliography), an eyewitness account of the events of April–July 1483, confirms More's narrative on many points.

coronation of the young prince and celebrate the new dynasty
that had developed from the union of the white and red roses,
yet in this very poem[9] he attacks the grasping methods of
Henry VII's agents, Empson and Dudley. More's indictment
of Richard III is not framed along the lines of party politics;
for him, Richard, however historical he may have been, was also
a symbol of the evils which permeate a kingdom when tyranny
is allowed to take the place of wise government and good order.
More's Richard is evil not because he is a Yorkist king but
because he is a dissimulating tyrant.

Tyranny, for the author of Utopia, was a fact of literature as
well as a fact of history, a subject for philosophical meditation
as well as an ever-present danger in a kingdom. More pondered
the problem throughout his career: in his early translations of
Lucian, where he wrote an original declamation on tyranni-
cide[10]; in a number of his Latin poems,[11] which are concerned,
like the *Utopia,* with "the best state of the commonwealth"; and
finally in his consideration of the limits of secular power, when,
as the king's prisoner in 1534–35, he analyzed his own case as
one in which "a man might lose his head and have no harm."
As his friend Erasmus remarked in 1519, Thomas More "had
always had a peculiar loathing for tyranny."

To read the *History* with these considerations in mind may
provide some answers, however partial, to the questions I posed
above. It may well be that More's own involvement, after
1517,[12] in the affairs of government left him little time for
literary or historical pursuits. Yet More must also have seen—
and this awareness may help to account for his leaving the
History unfinished and unpublished—that his work could easily
be read (as it has since so often been read) as an apology for the

9. For the text, see the first of the Latin poems in this edition.

10. *Translations of Lucian,* ed. C. R. Thompson (New Haven,
1974), Vol. 3, Part 1, in the Yale Edition of the Complete Works,
pp. 94–127.

11. Most of these are given, in English translation, in this volume.

12. The year More became a member of the royal council.

Tudors. More never doubted that tyranny could emerge in the new dynasty just as it had surfaced in the old one. As he told his son-in-law William Roper, after the latter had remarked on the affection Henry VIII showed him, "I may tell thee I have no cause to be proud thereof, for if my head could win him a castle in France, It should not fail to go."[13] The reality of Tudor *Machtpolitik* was never far from More's mind. He could, and did, live with it for a while, but he felt no need to sanction the powers-that-were by finishing, much less publishing, his *History* of the "tyrant" whom they had overthrown.

Thus the *Richard* remained, during More's lifetime, a kind of literary exercise. A few of his close friends, as the circulation of the English manuscripts suggest, probably read it, but for More himself, the text was essentially a private matter. He does not refer to it in any of his other writings, published or unpublished, but it stands nevertheless as a landmark in the development of sixteenth-century prose and as a remarkable witness to what the new humanist history could accomplish. Behind More's portrait of Richard lay the work of the classical historians, especially the Latin historians, Sallust, Suetonius, and above all, the newly discovered Tacitus.[14] From them More learned how to avoid the item-by-item, year-by-year method of historical writing that characterized the typical English chronicle of his day. His narrative is a proper monograph, concentrated on one brief period of time, the years of Richard III's usurpation of the throne. It thus draws to itself all of those dramatic qualities—the fictitious speeches, the stage directions, even a kind of five-act structure[15] —which can be found in Sallust and Tacitus and which were to prove so influential for the playwrights of the later century. As Roger Ascham was to write in 1553, More's *History* "doth so

13. *Life of More,* in *Two Early Tudor Lives,* ed. R. S. Sylvester and D. P. Harding (New Haven, 1962), p. 208.

14. For More's use of these authors as models, see *CW 2,* lxxx–civ.

15. These matters are excellently treated in A. N. Kincaid's article, "The Dramatic Structure of Sir Thomas More's *History of King Richard III,*" *Studies in English Literature, 12* (1972), 223–42.

content all men, as if the rest of our story of England were so
done, we might well compare with France, Italy, or Germany
in that behalf."[16]

At the verbal level of style, More rarely wrote more artfully
than he did in the *Richard*. Any one of the long speeches that
punctuate the rhythm of his narrative will well repay close
study:[17] Edward IV's dying words to his relatives and retainers
or his repartee with his mother over the question of his marriage
to Elizabeth Woodville, Buckingham's splendid tirade against
sanctuary men (and sanctuary children) or his notorious king-
making speech, twice delivered, before the assembly at the
Guildhall. More catches the modulations of colloquial idiom as
he shows the London citizens speculating upon the execution
of Hastings, but he can rise to grave and measured rhythms
when he tells the story of Jane Shore,[18] a story some men might
think "too slight a thing to be written of and set among the remembrances of great matters.... Her doings were not much
less [than those of "great" men], albeit they be much less remembered, because they were not so evil. For men use [are
accustomed], if they have an evil turn, to write it in marble, and
whoso doth us a good turn, we write it in dust; which is not
worst proved by her, for at this day she beggeth of many at this
day living, that at this day had begged if she had not been."

In the *History* itself the figure of Jane contrasts sharply with
that of the plotting protector. Her relative innocence, her hum-

16. *A Discourse of the Affairs of Germany,* in *English Works,* ed.
W. A. Wright (Cambridge, 1904), p. 126.

17. The reader may also wish to ponder the fact that most of
Richard's own speeches begin in indirect discourse and shift later to
direct; those of the other major characters are usually given directly.
An exception is, of course, the protector's staccato outburst of questions
in the Council in the Tower scene.

18. Most of what we know of Jane Shore is contained in More's
narrative and her story was to prove immensely popular in Elizabethan
verse, prose, and drama. The recent researches of Nicolas Barker have
provided a good deal of additional information, including the fact that
her maiden name was Elizabeth Lambert (see the Bibliography).

ble sacrificing of herself in the desires and interests of others, makes her the ideal foil to the scheming Richard, who presents himself, at this point in More's narrative, as a kind of divine savior, "sent out of heaven into this vicious world for the amendment of men's manners." Richard's world, as More imagines it for us, is indeed vicious. Cabals and sudden death are constant terrors. The protector and his cohorts present one face to the world and another to each other. Those who suffer under their machinations appear to be mere spectators at a play, watching a kind of impudent mime that may, at any moment, involve them in the action. Richard casts himself in role after role, but More never lets us doubt that men can see through his disguises. Each of the protector's triumphs turns on a piece of bad acting —during Shaa's sermon he actually misses his entrance cue—in which even the least of the citizens can discern that the role and the man do not square.

Much of the magnificent tension of More's prose in the *History* arises from these dramatized conflicts between public show and private perception. Irony is everywhere and our sense of danger is only heightened by our growing awareness that we ought to be able to laugh at Richard even as we shudder at his calculated crimes. More never quite takes the final step into farce (this, some would say, was left for Shakespeare to effect), but he does focus all the ambivalent elements in one great metaphor that caps the scene in which Richard, after twice refusing the crown, at last accepts it. The formalities take place as "in a stage play" where the shoemaker may, for an hour, become a sultan, acting out his role in the insubstantial pageant. Yet everyone knows, though they dare not speak, that the assumed character is not the real one. The game, as Richard plays it, is a royal pastime, but it is also, as he will discover and as More's brilliant pun upon the word "scaffolds" makes clear, a game of death that can bring only terror to the realm which it would ostensibly serve. "And so they said that these matters be kings' games, as it were, stage plays, and for the more part played upon scaffolds, in which poor men be but the lookers-on. And they that wise be, will meddle no farther. For they that sometime step up and play with them, when they cannot play their parts, they disorder the play and do themself no good." Perhaps, when the final act is concluded, the wisest men prove to be not those who remain aloof from the drama, but rather those who, like More himself, accept a part and play it well, realizing as they do so the full context of their role and the probable consequences of their choice.

In addition to the *History of Richard III,* this volume in the modernized series of More's works presents a selection from his English and (in translation) his Latin poems. In the English selections I have not included More's rhyme-royal stanzas upon Fortune or his verse paraphrases of Pico della Mirandola's "Twelve Rules for a Man in Spiritual Battle."[19] The poems appearing here show that More approached the writing of verse with the same experimental spirit he brought to the composition of the *Richard.* The "Merry Jest," probably written about 1503 and perhaps recited as part of the festivities celebrating the appointment of John More, More's father, as a sergeant of the law, takes up a popular verse rhythm with rollicking energy. For all its fun, the poem has serious undertones: not every rising young lawyer is likely to enjoy himself so hugely at the expense of his chosen profession. What role should a man play and how should he play it? The comic consequences of the sergeant's disguise need not obscure the fact that young More, here as elsewhere, was meditating deeply upon the choice of life open to him.

The "Pageant Verses," designed to serve as *tituli* (inscriptions) beneath the tapestries in his father's house, also show

19. Both of these groups of verses, with the remainder of the English Poems, are scheduled for publication as Volume 1 in the Yale Edition of the Complete Works. The Fortune poems are excellently treated by H. Schulte Herbrüggen, "Sir Thomas Mores Fortuna-Verse," in *Lebende Antike, Symposium für Rudolf Sühnel* (Berlin, 1967) pp. 155–72.

More at work structuring experience into meaningful patterns. Themes from Petrarch's *Trionfi* mingle and blend with the Seven Ages of Man *topos* so much beloved by antiquity and the middle ages. Youth yields to Manhood, Age to Death, Fame and Time to Eternity. The seven-line vignettes are deftly etched, still points in the inexorable temporal process which can be controlled only by the Poet (the final pageant) whose fictive images provide elusive glimpses of the Creator Himself. In his "Rueful Lamentation" at the death of Queen Elizabeth (1503), More tested his hand at elegy, hitting felicitously upon the dramatic device of the Queen's pronouncing her own lament. Once more the transience of life is the central theme as Elizabeth surveys the world, with all its glories, which she has now left. More's poem challenges comparison with the "tragedies" of the *Mirror for Magistrates* fifty years later and, in its restrained dignity, it need yield nothing to any of the *Mirror* poets. Finally, "Lewis the Lost Lover" and "Davey the Dicer" show More returning, while a prisoner in the Tower, to a pastime—the making of verses—which he had not enjoyed for many years.

Of all More's English poems, only the "Merry Jest" and the Pico verses were published during his lifetime. As a Latin poet, however, his fame was great and long-lasting.[20] The Epigrams, probably composed sporadically between 1497 and 1517, were first published in 1518. About 100 of the 260 extant poems are translations from the *Greek Anthology,* literary exercises in which More perfected the style and meters he was to use so successfully in his original efforts. Contemporaries praised the Epigrams, not only for their moral purity, but also for their wide range of subject matter. More does include a few bawdy pieces, but he never attempts to rival the erotic sensuousness of the Italian Neo-Latin poets, much less the frequent "saltiness"

20. As is shown by the large number of allusions to and imitations and translations of the *Epigrammata* that survive from the sixteenth and seventeenth centuries. For a partial listing, see R. W. Gibson and J. M. Patrick, *St. Thomas More: A Preliminary Bibliography of His Works and of Moreana to the Year 1750* (New Haven, 1961).

of Martial. Instead he writes, among the original poems, a series
on politics and the best form of government; he attacks astrologers and quack doctors, satirizes a worldly or an ignorant clergy,
engages in a spirited exchange with a French poetaster, medi-
tates upon fate, advises Candidus on how to choose a wife and
consoles Sabinus on not being able to control his, translates English songs into Latin verse, and pens a fine group of occasional
poems which reflect warmly and humanely on the course his
many friendships had taken. In selecting some fifty of the Latin
poems, I have tried to choose the best, but I have also attempted
to illustrate the range which the series as a whole embraces.
Translations can never substitute for the originals, but they can
capture something of the pointed wit and shrewd observation
that give the *Epigrammata* a minor but well-deserved place in
Latin literature.

A NOTE ON THE TEXT

The text of the *History of King Richard III* presented here
is based on that given in Volume 2 of the Yale Edition of the
Complete Works (ed. R. S. Sylvester, New Haven, 1963). Spelling and punctuation have been modernized and glosses have
been provided for words which have changed their meaning or
become archaic since the early sixteenth century. Where archaic
words occur frequently in the text, glosses have been repeated at
fairly regular intervals. Brief historical notes, including correc-
tions of More's occasional errors in assigning Christian names,
are interwoven with the glosses. When William Rastell printed
More's *History* in *The English Works* of 1557, he enlarged his
holograph text by adding to it three passages which he translated from a manuscript copy of More's Latin *Historia*. I have
not deleted these passages[21] from the present edition.

21. The translations occur on the following pages: 39 ("And if
examples . . . his brother since"), 42–44 "When the protector . . . other
noble men"), and 83–84 ("The next day . . . coronation of his
nephew").

The text of the English poems presented here is the old spelling version as it will appear in Volume 1 of the Yale Edition of the Complete Works. I have modernized the use of long *s* and have adjusted *u* and *v*, *i* and *j* to modern practice. Punctuation and capitalization follow the originals, except for a few emendations of obvious errors. To have modernized the spelling and punctuation of the poems would have been to tamper unduly with More's meter and diction. Glosses are provided on the same principles as those adopted for the *History*.

The translations of the Latin poems are those of Leicester Bradner and Charles Arthur Lynch. In a few places they embody revisions made since the first appearance of their edition in 1953.[22] Each of the Latin poems is identified in a footnote by its Bradner-Lynch number, cited as "*BL*." The abbreviation "*AP*" in the footnotes to the epigrams refers to the Anthologia Palatina text of the Greek Anthology.

R. S. Sylvester

New Haven, Connecticut
May 1975

---

22. *The Latin Epigrams of Thomas More* (Chicago, 1953). A revised and enlarged version of this edition will comprise Volume 3, Part 2, in the Yale Edition of More's Complete Works.

BIBLIOGRAPHY

The following list of books is designed to serve as a guide for further reading and to supplement the information supplied in the Introduction and footnotes. I have tried to include most of the important work done on the reign of Richard III since 1963, but the Bibliography is necessarily selective and the interested student should also consult Conyers Read, *A Bibliography of British History,* 2d ed. (Oxford, 1959), and Mortimer Levine, *Tudor England 1485–1603* (Cambridge, 1968). Current research on Thomas More is regularly calendared in the periodical *Moreana,* Vols. 1–12 et seq., 1963–.

I. TEXTS

The following volumes have already appeared in the Yale Edition of the Complete Works of St. Thomas More (New Haven and London, 1961–).

Vol. 2, *The History of King Richard III,* ed. R. S. Sylvester, 1963. Cited as *CW 2.*

Vol. 3, Part 1, *Translations of Lucian,* ed. C. R. Thompson, 1974.

Vol. 4, *Utopia,* ed. E. Surtz and J. H. Hexter, 1965. Cited as *CW 4.*

Vol. 5, *Responsio ad Lutherum,* ed. J. M. Headley, 1969.

Vol. 8, *The Confutation of Tyndale's Answer,* ed. L. A. Schuster, R. C. Marius, J. P. Lusardi, and R. J. Schoeck, 1973.

Three additional volumes (Vol. 12, *A Dialogue of Comfort;* Vol. 13, *Treatise on the Passion,* etc.; and Vol. 14, *De Tristitia*

Christi) are in press and are scheduled for publication in 1976. It is expected that the entire series will be completed by 1985.

Two companion volumes to the Edition are:

R. W. Gibson and J. M. Patrick, *St. Thomas More: A Preliminary Bibliography of His Works and of Moreana to the Year 1750*, 1961.

Thomas More's Prayerbook, ed. L. L. Martz and R. S. Sylvester, 1969.

In the Selected Works of St. Thomas More series, the following modern-spelling texts are available in both clothbound and paperbound editions:

E. F. Rogers, ed., *St. Thomas More: Selected Letters*, 1961.

E. Surtz, ed., *Utopia*, 1964.

The standard edition of More's correspondence is E. F. Rogers, ed., *The Correspondence of Sir Thomas More* (Princeton, 1947). An expanded and revised edition of this volume will be published as Volume 15 of the Yale Edition, ed. H. Schulte Herbrüggen.

II. BIOGRAPHIES

A. Sixteenth and Seventeenth Centuries

William Roper, *The Lyfe of Sir Thomas Moore, knighte* (1557), ed. E. V. Hitchcock, London, 1935, Early English Text Society. Roper's *Life*, together with Cavendish's *Life of Wolsey*, is conveniently available in paperback in *Two Early Tudor Lives*, ed. R. S. Sylvester and D. P. Harding, New Haven, 1962.

Nicholas Harpsfield, *The Life and Death of Sir Thomas Moore, knight* (1557), ed. E. V. Hitchcock and R. W. Chambers, London, 1932, Early English Text Society.

Thomas Stapleton, as Part III of his *Tres Thomae, The Life and Illustrious Martyrdom of Sir Thomas More* (1588), trans. P. E. Hallett ,1928, rev. ed. by E. E. Reynolds, London, 1966.

Ro. Ba., *The Lyfe of Syr Thomas More* (1599), ed. E. V. Hitchcock, P. E. Hallett, and A. W. Reed, London, 1950, Early English Text Society. (The author is not identified.)

Cresacre More, *The Life and Death of Sir Thomas More* (1626–31). The last of the family biographies, written by More's great-grandson. A modern edition is being prepared by Michael Anderegg.

B. Modern Biographies

T. E. Bridgett, *Life and Writings of Blessed Thomas More,* London, 1891, 3d ed. 1904.

R. W. Chambers, *Thomas More,* London, 1935.

E. E. Reynolds, *The Field is Won,* London, 1968.

G. Marc'hadour, *Thomas More ou la sage folie,* Paris, 1971.

R. S. Sylvester, ed., *St. Thomas More: Action and Contemplation* (essays by R. J. Schoeck, G. Elton, L. L. Martz, and G. Marc'hadour), New Haven, 1972.

III. STUDIES AND COMPLEMENTARY MATERIALS

André, Bernard, "Vita Henrici VII," in *Memorials of King Henry the Seventh,* ed. James Gairdner, London, 1858.

Barker, Nicolas, and Birley, Sir Robert, "The Story of Jane Shore," *Etoniana,* nos. 125–26 (June 4 and December 2, 1972), pp. 383–414.

Berdan, John, *Early Tudor Poetry,* New York, 1920. Reprint, Hamden, Conn., 1961.

Bradner, L., *Musae Anglicanae,* London, 1940.

Buc, George, *The History of the Life and Reigne of Richard the Third,* London, 1646.

The Cely Papers, ed. H. E. Malden, London, Camden Society, 3d series, *I* (1900).

Chrimes, S. B., *Henry VII,* London, 1972.

Churchill, George B., "Richard the Third up to Shakespeare," *Palaestra, 10* (1900).

Dean, Leonard F., "Literary Problems in More's *Richard III,*" *PMLA, 58* (1943), 22–41.

Gairdner, James, *Richard the Third,* 3d ed., Cambridge, 1898.

Hammond, E. P., *English Verse between Chaucer and Surrey,* Durham, N.C., 1927.

Hanham, Alison, "Richard III, Lord Hastings and the Historians," *English Historical Review, 343* (April 1972), 233–48.

Hudson, H. H., *The English Epigram in the Renaissance,* Princeton, 1947.

Hutton, James, *The Greek Anthology in France,* Ithaca, 1946.

Hutton, James, *The Greek Anthology in Italy,* Ithaca, 1935.

Jacob, E. F., *The Fifteenth Century,* Oxford, 1961.

Kendall, P. M., *Richard the Third,* New York, 1955.

Kincaid, Arthur N., "The Dramatic Structure of Sir Thomas More's *History of King Richard III,*" *Studies in English Literature, 12* (1972), 223–42.

Kingsford, C. L., *English Historical Literature in the Fifteenth Century,* Oxford, 1913.

Lander, J. R., "The Treason and Death of the Duke of Clarence: A Re-Interpretation," *Canadian Journal of History, 2* (1967), 1–28.

Lander, J. R., *The Wars of the Roses,* London, 1965.

Letters and Papers, Foreign and Domestic, of the Reigns of Richard III and Henry VII, ed. James Gairdner, 2 vols., London, 1861 and 1863.

Levy, F. J., *Tudor Historical Thought,* San Marino, Calif., 1967.

McKisack, May, *Medieval History in the Tudor Age,* Oxford, 1971.

Mancini, Dominic, *The Usurpation of Richard the Third,* ed. C. A. J. Armstrong, 2d rev. ed., Oxford, 1969.

Mann, Wolfgang, *Lateinische Dichtung in England,* Halle, 1939.

Marsden, J. H., *Philomorus, Notes on the Latin Poems of Sir Thomas More,* 2d ed., London, 1878.

Materials for a History of the Reign of Henry VII, ed. William Campbell, 2 vols., London, 1873 and 1877.

Myers, A. R., "The Character of Richard III," *History Today, 4* (1954), 511–21.

Myers, A. R., ed., *The Household of Edward IV,* Liverpool, 1959.

Myers, A. R., "Household of Queen Elizabeth Woodville 1466–67," *Bulletin of the John Rylands Library, 50* (1967), 207–35.

Pollard, A. F., "The Lamentation of Queen Elisabeth," *Times Literary Supplement, 31* (1932), 499.

Pollard, A. F., "The Making of Sir Thomas More's *Richard III,*" in *Historical Essays in Honour of James Tait,* Manchester, 1933, pp. 223–38.

Pollard, A. F., "Sir Thomas More's *Richard III,*" *History, 17* (1933), 317–23.

Pyle, Fitzroy, "Sir Thomas More's Verse Rhythms," *Times Literary Supplement, 36* (1937), p. 76.

Ramsay, J. H., *Lancaster and York,* 2 vols., Oxford, 1892.

Rhodes, D. E., *John Argentine, Provost of King's, His Life and Library.* Amsterdam, 1967.

Rowse, A. L., *Bosworth Field and the Wars of the Roses,* London, 1966.

Scofield, Cora L., *The Life and Reign of Edward the Fourth,* 2 vols., London, 1923.

The Stonor Letters and Papers, ed. C. L. Kingsford, London, Camden Society, 3d series, 29–30 (1919).

Storey, R. L., *The End of the House of Lancaster,* London, 1966.

Sylvester, R. S., "A Part of His Own: Thomas More's Literary Personality in His Early Works," *Moreana, 15–16* (1967), 29–42.

Tanner, L., *Recollections of a Westminster Antiquary,* London, 1969.

Tanner, L. E., and Wright, W., "Recent Investigations regarding the Fate of the Princes in the Tower," *Archaeologia, 84* (1934), 1–26.

Tudor-Craig, Pamela, *Richard III* (a descriptive catalogue of the exhibition held at the National Portrait Gallery, 27 June–7 October, 1973), London, 1973.

Weiss, R., *Humanism in England during the Fifteenth Century,* 3d ed., Oxford, 1967.

Willow, M. E., *An Analysis of the English Poems of St. Thomas More,* Nieuwkoop, 1974.

Wood, Charles T., "The Deposition of Edward V," *Traditio,* *31* (1975), 247–86.

THE HISTORY
OF
KING RICHARD THE THIRD

The history of King Richard the Third (unfinished), written by Master Thomas More, then one of the under-sheriffs of London, about the year of our Lord 1513. Which work hath been before this time printed in Harding's Chronicle and in Hall's Chronicle,[1] but very much corrupt in many places, sometime having less, and sometime having more, and altered in words and whole sentences, much varying fro the copy of his own hand, by[2] which this is printed.

King Edward, of that name the Fourth, after that he had lived fifty and three years, seven months, and six days, and thereof reigned two and twenty years, one month, and eight days,[3] died at Westminster the ninth day of April, the year of our redemption, a thousand four hundred four score and three, leaving much fair issue,[4] that is to wit, Edward the Prince, a thirteen year of age; Richard Duke of York, two year younger; Elizabeth, whose fortune and grace was after to be queen, wife

1. *Harding's . . . Hall's:* For these earlier printings of More's *History,* see the Introduction, p. xii.
2. from.
3. Edward IV (1442–83) had in fact reached the age of forty years, eleven months, and twelve days when he died. His coronation took place on June 28, 1461; he had already been popularly proclaimed as king on the previous March 1.
4. Edward, Prince of Wales (b. 1470), reigned as Edward V for only two months. Richard, Duke of York was probably born in 1473. Elizabeth of York (1466–1503) married Henry VII on January 18, 1486, but was not crowned queen until November 25, 1487. Cecily (1469–1507), after two previous royal betrothals, married Viscount Welles. (Her second marriage to a Lincolnshire man was never recognized by her family.) Bridget (1480?–1517?) entered a Dominican Convent in 1492. Anne (1475–1511) married Thomas Howard II in 1495. Katherine (1479–1527) married Lord William Courtenay before October 1495. More himself participated in the settlement of her husband's estate (1511–13).

unto King Henry the Seventh, and mother unto the Eighth; Cecily, not so fortunate as fair; Bridget, which, representing the virtue of her whose name she bare, professed and observed a religious life in Dartford, a house of close[5] nuns; Anne, that was after honorably married unto Thomas, then Lord Howard and after Earl of Surrey.[6] And Katherine which long time tossed in either fortune, sometime in wealth, oft in adversity, at the last, if this be the last, for yet she liveth, is by the benignity of her nephew, King Henry the Eighth, in very prosperous estate and worthy her birth and virtue.

This noble prince deceased at his palace of Westminster, and with great funeral honor and heaviness[7] of his people from thence conveyed, was interred at Windsor.[8] A king of such governance and behavior in time of peace (for in war each party must needs be other's enemy) that there was never any prince of this land attaining the crown by battle so heartily beloved with the substaunce[9] of the people, nor he himself so specially in any part of his life, as at the time of his death. Which favor and affection, yet after his decease, by the cruelty, mischief, and trouble of the tempestuous world that followed, highly toward him more increased. At such time as he died, the displeasure of those that bare him grudge, for King Henry's sake the Sixth, whom he deposed,[1] was well assuaged, and, in effect, quenched, in that that many of them were dead in more than twenty years of his reign, a great part of a long life. And many of them in the mean season grown into his favor, of which he was never strange.[2] He was a goodly personage, and very princely to behold: of heart courageous, politic[3] in counsel, in adversity

5. cloistered.
6. Thomas Howard II, third Duke of Norfolk (1473–1554), did not become Earl of Surrey until February 1, 1514, a fact which helps to fix the date of More's *History*.
7. sadness.   8. on April 19, 1483.   9. the greater part.
1. King Henry VI (1422–71) was deposed in 1461; restored by the Earl of Warwick in 1470, he died in the Tower, May 21–22, 1471.
2. sparing.   3. prudent.

nothing abashed, in prosperity rather joyful than proud, in peace just and merciful, in war sharp and fierce, in the field bold and hardy, and nevertheless—no farther than wisdom would—adventurous. Whose wars who so well consider, he shall no less commend his wisdom where he voided[4] than his manhood where he vanquished.

He was of visage lovely, of body mighty, strong, and clean made,[5] howbeit in his later days with over-liberal diet somewhat corpulent and burly, and nevertheless not uncomely; he was of youth greatly given to fleshly wantonness, from which health of body in great prosperity and fortune, without a special grace, hardly refraineth. This fault not greatly grieved the people, for neither could any one man's pleasure stretch and extend to the displeasure of very many, and was without violence, and, over that, in his later days, lessened and well left. In which time of his later days, this realm was in quiet and prosperous estate: no fear of outward enemies, no war in hand, nor none toward,[6] but such as no man looked for; the people toward the prince not in a constrained fear, but in a willing and loving obedience; among themself, the commons in good peace. The lords whom he knew at variance, himself in his deathbed appeased. He had left all gathering of money[7] (which is the only thing that withdraweth the hearts of Englishmen fro the prince) nor any thing intended he to take in hand, by which he should be driven thereto, for his tribute out of France[8] he had before obtained. And the year foregoing his death, he had obtained Berwick.[9] And albeit that all the time of his reign, he was with his people

4. withdrew, refrained from entering into.
5. *clean made:* well proportioned.   6. impending.
7. Edward had in fact just levied a tax for a new campaign against the Scots.
8. *tribute...France:* The annual pension of 50,000 crowns obtained by Edward from Louis XI in the Treaty of Picquigny (August 29, 1475).
9. Berwick Castle, taken from the Scots by Richard of Gloucester's troops on August 24, 1482.

so benign, courteous, and so familiar that no part of his virtues was more esteemed, yet that condition[1] in the end of his days (in which many princes by a long continued sovereignty decline into a proud port[2] from debonair[3] behavior of their beginning) marvelously in him grew and increased, so far forth that in the summer, the last that ever he saw, his highness, being at Windsor in hunting, sent for the mayor[4] and aldermen of London to him, for none other errand but to have them hunt and be merry with him, where he made them not so stately, but so friendly and so familiar cheer, and sent venison from thence so freely into the city, that no one thing in many days before gat[5] him either more hearts or more hearty favor among the common people, which oftentimes more esteem and take for greater kindness a little courtesy than a great benefit.

So deceased (as I have said) this noble king, in that time in which his life was most desired. Whose love of his people and their entire affection toward him had been to his noble children (having in themself also as many gifts of nature, as many princely virtues, as much goodly towardness[6] as their age could receive) a marvelous fortress and sure armor, if division and dissension of their friends had not unarmed them and left them destitute, and the execrable desire of sovereignty provoked him to their destruction, which if either kind[7] or kindness had holden place, must needs have been their chief defense. For Richard the Duke of Gloucester,[8] by nature their uncle, by office their protector,[9] to their father beholden, to them self by oath and allegiance bounden, all the bands broken that binden man and man together, without any respect of God or the world, un-

1. quality.   2. bearing.   3. gracious.
4. William Heryot or Haryott.   5. got.
6. natural aptitude.   7. kinship.
8. Richard (1452–1485) had been created Duke of Gloucester in June 1461.
9. Probably named protector in Edward's will, Richard was formally appointed by the Council after he arrived in London.

naturally contrived to bereave them,[1] not only their dignity, but also their lives. But forasmuch as this duke's demeanor ministreth[2] in effect all the whole matter whereof this book shall entreat,[3] it is therefore convenient somewhat to show you, ere we farther go, what manner of man this was that could find in his heart so much mischief to conceive.

Richard Duke of York,[4] a noble man and a mighty, began not by war, but by law, to challenge the crown, putting his claim into the parliament, where his cause was either for right or favor so far forth advanced that King Henry his blood (albeit he had a goodly prince)[5] utterly rejected; the crown was by authority of parliament entailed unto the Duke of York and his issue male in remainder immediately after the death of King Henry.[6] But the duke not enduring so long to tarry, but intending, under pretext of dissension and debate arising in the realm, to prevent[7] his time and to take upon him the rule in King Harry his life, was with many nobles of the realm at Wakefield[8] slain, leaving three sons—Edward, George, and Richard. All three as they were great states[9] of birth, so were they great and stately of stomach,[1] greedy and ambitious of authority, and impatient of partners. Edward, revenging his father's death, deprived King Henry and attained the crown. George Duke of Clarence[2] was a goodly noble prince, and at all points fortunate, if either his

---

1. *bereave them:* i.e., bereave them of.
2. *demeanor ministreth:* behavior furnishes.   3. treat.
4. Richard, Duke of York (1411–60) only son of Richard, Earl of Cambridge by Anne Mortimer, claimed descent from Edward III through both of his parents.
5. Edward (1453–71) slain at the Battle of Tewkesbury.
6. The compromise between the Houses of York and Lancaster was effected on October 31, 1460. But the duke soon began to raise an army against Henry VI.
7. act before.   8. The Battle of Wakefield, December 30, 1460.
9. noblemen.   1. *stately of stomach:* haughty in disposition.
2. Clarence (1449–78) had accused the queen of necromancy in the death of his wife and had been secretly executed in the Tower.

own ambition had not set him against his brother, or the envy of his enemies his brother against him. For were it by the queen[3] and the lords of her blood which highly maligned the king's kindred (as women commonly, not of malice, but of nature, hate them whom their husbands love), or were it a proud appetite of the duke himself intending to be king, at the least wise heinous treason was there laid to his charge, and finally, were he faulty, were he faultless, attainted was he by parliament and judged to the death, and thereupon hastily drowned in a butt of malmsey;[4] whose death King Edward (albeit he commanded it) when he wist[5] it was done, piteously bewailed and sorrowfully repented.

Richard, the third son, of whom we now entreat, was in wit and courage equal with either of them, in body and prowess far under them both: little of stature, ill-featured of limbs, crookbacked, his left shoulder much higher than his right, hard favored[6] of visage, and such as is in states[7] called warly,[8] in other men otherwise. He was malicious, wrathful, envious, and from afore his birth, ever froward.[9] It is for truth reported that the duchess his mother[1] had so much ado in her travail,[2] that she could not be delivered of him uncut, and that he came into the world with the feet forward, as men be borne outward,[3] and (as the fame runneth) also not untoothed—whether men of hatred report above the truth, or else that nature changed her course in his beginning, which in the course of his life many things unnaturally committed. None evil[4] captain was he in the war, as to which his disposition was more meetly[5] than for peace. Sundry victories had he, and sometime overthrows, but never in default as for his own person, either of hardiness or politic order.

---

3. Elizabeth Woodville (1437–92).   4. a strong, sweet wine.
5. knew.
6. *hard favored:* ugly.   7. noblemen.   8. warlike.
9. perverse.   1. Cecily, Duchess of York (d. 1495).
2. labor (when Richard was born).
3. *borne outward:* carried out of this world (at their funerals).
4. *None evil:* no unskilled.   5. suited.

Free was he called of dispense, and somewhat above his power
liberal; with large gifts he get[6] him unsteadfast friendship, for
which he was fain to pill[7] and spoil in other places and get him
steadfast hatred. He was close and secret, a deep dissimuler,[8]
lowly of countenance, arrogant of heart, outwardly coumpin-
able[9] where he inwardly hated, not letting[1] to kiss whom he
thought to kill; dispiteous[2] and cruel, not for evil will alway,
but ofter for ambition, and either for the surety or increase of
his estate. Friend and foe was much what indifferent:[3] where
his advantage grew, he spared no man's death whose life with-
stood his purpose. He slew with his own hands King Henry the
Sixth, being prisoner in the Tower, as men constantly say, and
that without commandment or knowledge of the king,[4] which
would undoubtedly, if he had intended that thing, have appointed that butcherly office to some other than his own born
brother. Some wise men also ween[5] that his drift[6] covertly conveyed, lacked not in helping forth his brother of Clarence to his
death, which he resisted[7] openly, howbeit somewhat (as men
deemed) more faintly than he that were heartily minded to his
wealth.[8] And they that thus deem think that he long time in
King Edward's life forethought to be king in case that the king
his brother (whose life he looked that evil diet should shorten),
should happen to decease (as indeed he did) while his children
were young. And they deem that for this intent he was glad of
his brother's death, the Duke of Clarence, whose life must needs
have hindered him so intending; whether the same Duke of
Clarence had kept him true to his nephew, the young king, or
enterprised to be king himself.

But of all this point is there no certainty, and whoso divineth
upon conjectures may as well shoot too far as too short.
Howbeit, this have I by credible information learned, that the

6. got.   7. pillage.   8. dissembler.   9. friendly.
1. hesitating.   2. spiteful.
3. *Friend . . . indifferent:* i.e., he treated friend and foe impartially.
4. i.e., Edward IV.   5. think.   6. scheming.   7. denied.
8. *his wealth:* Clarence's welfare.

self[9] night in which King Edward died, one Mistlebrook,[1] long
ere morning, came in great haste to the house of one Potter[2]
dwelling in Redcross Street without Cripplegate; and when he
was with hasty rapping quickly letten in, he showed unto Potter
that King Edward was departed. "By my troth, man," quod
Potter, "then will my master, the Duke of Gloucester, be king."
What cause he had so to think, hard it is to say—whether he
being toward[3] him anything knew that he such thing purposed,
or otherwise had any inkling thereof, for he was not likely to
speak it of nought.[4]

But now to return to the course of this history: Were it that
the Duke of Gloucester had of old foreminded[5] this conclusion,
or was now at erst[6] thereunto moved and put in hope by the occasion of the tender age of the young princes, his nephews (as
opportunity and likelihood of speed[7] putteth a man in courage
of that he never intended), certain is it that he contrived their
destruction, with the usurpation of the regal dignity upon himself. And forasmuch as he well wist and holp[8] to maintain a long
continued grudge and heart brenning[9] between the queen's
kindred and the king's blood, either party envying other's authority, he now thought that their division should be (as it was
indeed) a fortherly[1] beginning to the pursuit of his intent and a
sure ground for the foundation of all his building, if he might
first, under the pretext of revenging of old displeasure, abuse
the anger and ignorance of the one party to the destruction of
the other, and then win to his purpose as many as he could, and
those that could not be won might be lost ere they looked there-

9. same, very.
1. Probably William Mistlebrook (d. 1513) who had been Edward
IV's servant and auditor of numerous crown lands.
2. Probably Richard Potter, one of Richard's servants, appointed an
Attorney in Chancery in 1483.
3. in attendance upon.   4. *of nought:* without good cause.
5. intended.
6. *at erst:* first.   7. success.   8. helped.
9. *heart brenning:* heated jealousy.   1. favorable.

for.[2] For of one thing was he certain, that if his intent were perceived, he should soon have made peace between the both parties with his own blood.

King Edward in his life, albeit that this dissension between his friends somewhat irked him, yet in his good health he somewhat the less regarded it because he thought whatsoever business should fall between them, himself should alway be able to rule both the parties. But in his last sickness,[3] when he perceived his natural strength so sore enfeebled that he despaired all recovery, then he, considering the youth of his children—albeit he nothing less mistrusted than that that happened, yet well foreseeing that many harms might grow by their debate while the youth of his children should lack discretion of themself and good counsel of their friends, of which either party should counsel for their own commodity[4] and rather by pleasant advice to win themselves favor, than by profitable advertisement[5] to do the children good—he called some of them before him that were at variance, and in especial the Lord Marquis Dorset,[6] the queen's son by her first husband, and Richard[7] the Lord Hastings, a noble man, then lord chamberlain, against whom the queen specially grudged for the great favor the king bare him, and also for that she thought him secretly familiar with the king in wanton company. Her kindred also bare him sore,[8] as well for that the king had made him captain of Calais (which office the Lord Rivers,[9] brother to the queen, claimed of the king's former promise), as for divers other great gifts which he received that they looked for.

2. for it.
3. Edward's last illness, the nature of which is disputed, began about Easter (March 30, 1483).   4. advantage.   5. instruction.
6. Thomas Grey, Lord Ferrers (c. 1456–1501).
7. Actually, *William* Lord Hastings (1431–83), a strong supporter of Edward IV. He had been granted the lieutenancy of Calais in 1471.
8. *bare him sore:* strongly disliked him.
9. Anthony Woodville, Baron Scales and second Earl Rivers (1442?–83).

When these lords with divers other of both the parties were come in presence, the king, lifting up himself and underset[1] with pillows, as it is reported, on this wise said unto them: "My lords, my dear kinsmen and allies, in what plight I lie you see and I feel. By which, the less while I look to live with you, the more deeply am I moved to care in what case[2] I leave you; for such as I leave you, such be my children like to find you. Which if they should (that God forbid) find you at variance, might hap to fall themself at war ere their discretion would serve to set you at peace. Ye see their youth, of which I reckon the only surety to rest in your concord. For it sufficeth not that all you love them, if each of you hate other. If they were men, your faithfulness haply[3] would suffice. But childhood must be maintained by men's authority and slipper[4] youth underpropped with elder counsel, which neither they can have but[5] ye give it, nor ye give it, if ye gree[6] not. For where each laboreth to break that the other maketh, and for hatred of each other's person impugneth each other's counsel, there must it needs be long ere any good conclusion go forward. And also while either party laboreth to be chief, flattery shall have more place than plain and faithful advice, of which must needs ensue the evil bringing up of the prince, whose mind in tender youth infect,[7] shall readily fall to mischief and riot, and draw down with this noble realm to ruin; but if[8] grace turn him to wisdom, which if God send, then they that by evil means before pleased him best, shall after fall farthest out of favor, so that ever at length evil drifts drive to nought and good plain ways prosper. Great variance hath there long been between you, not always for great causes. Sometime a thing right well intended, our misconstruction turneth unto worse, or a small displeasure done us, either our own affection[9] or evil tongues agrieveth.[1]

"But this wot[2] I well: ye never had so great cause of hatred as

---

1. propped up.   2. condition.   3. perhaps.   4. unstable.
5. unless.   6. agree.   7. tainted.   8. *but if:* unless.
9. biased feeling.   1. exaggerate.   2. know.

ye have of love. That we be all men, that we be Christian men, this shall I leave for preachers to tell you (and yet I wot never whether any preacher's words ought more to move you than his that is by and by going to the place that they all preach of). But this shall I desire you to remember, that the one part of you is of my blood, the other of mine allies, and each of you with other, either of kindred or affinity,[3] which spiritual kindred of affinity, if the sacraments of Christ's church bear that weight with us that would God they did, should no less move us to charity than the respect of fleshly consanguinity. Our Lord forbid that you love together the worse for the self[4] cause that you ought to love the better. And yet that happeneth. And nowhere find we so deadly debate as among them which by nature and law most ought to agree together. Such a pestilent serpent is ambition and desire of vainglory and sovereignty, which among states[5] where he once entereth creepeth forth so far, till with division and variance he turneth all to mischief—first longing to be next the best, afterward equal with the best, and at last chief and above the best. Of which immoderate appetite of worship, and thereby of debate and dissension, what loss, what sorrow, what trouble hath within these few years grown in this realm, I pray God as well forget as we well remember. Which things if I could as well have foreseen, as I have with my more pain than pleasure proved,[6] by God's blessed lady (that was ever his oath) I would never have won the courtesy of men's knees with the loss of so many heads.

"But sithen[7] things past cannot be gaincalled,[8] much ought we the more beware, by what occasion we have taken so great hurt afore, that we eftsoons[9] fall not in that occasion again. Now be those griefs past, and all is (God be thanked) quiet and likely right well to prosper in wealthful peace under your cousins,[1] my

---

3. relationship by marriage.   4. very.   5. noblemen.
6. learned by experience.   7. since.
8. *gaincalled:* brought back again.   9. a second time.
1. used loosely to refer to any blood relative.

children, if God send them life and you love. Of which two things, the less loss were they by whom though God did His pleasure,[2] yet should the realm alway find kings and peradventure as good kings. But if you among yourself in a child's reign fall at debate, many a good man shall perish and haply he too, and ye too, ere this land find peace again. Wherefore, in these last words that ever I look to speak with you, I exhort you and require you all, for the love that you have ever borne to me, for the love that I have ever borne to you, for the love that our Lord beareth to us all, from this time forward, all griefs forgotten, each of you love other. Which I verily trust you will, if ye anything earthly regard—either God or your king, affinity or kindred, this realm, your own country, or your own surety."

And therewithal, the king no longer enduring to sit up, laid him down on his right side, his face toward them, and none was there present that could refrain from weeping. But the lords recomforting[3] him with as good words as they could and answering, for the time, as they thought to stand with his pleasure, there in his presence (as by their words appeared) each forgave other and joined their hands together, when (as it after appeared by their deeds) their hearts were far asunder.

As soon as the king was departed, the noble prince, his son, drew toward London, which at the time of his decease, kept his household at Ludlow in Wales.[4] Which country, being far off from the law and recourse to justice, was begun to be far out of good will and waxen[5] wild, robbers and reivers[6] walking at liberty uncorrected. And for this encheason[7] the prince was in the life of his father sent thither, to the end that the authority of his presence should refrain[8] evil disposed persons fro the boldness of their former outrages; to the governance and ordering of this young prince, at his sending thither, was there appointed

2. *they ... pleasure:* i.e., if they (the princes) should die of natural causes.   3. consoling.
4. Ludlow Castle, where Prince Edward had been sent in 1473 and where he heard of the king's death on April 14, 1483. He did not leave Ludlow for London until April 24.
5. grown.   6. thieves.   7. reason.   8. hold back, restrain.

Sir Anthony Woodville, Lord Rivers and brother unto the queen, a right honorable man, as valiant of hand as politic[9] in counsel. Adjoined were there unto him other of the same party, and, in effect, every one as he was nearest of kin unto the queen, so was planted next about the prince.[1]

That drift, by the queen not unwisely devised, whereby her blood might of youth be rooted in the prince's favor,[2] the Duke of Gloucester turned unto their destruction, and upon that ground set the foundation of all his unhappy building. For whomsoever he perceived either at variance with them or bearing himself their favor, he brake[3] unto them, some by mouth, some by writing and secret messengers, that it neither was reason nor in any wise to be suffered that the young king, their master and kinsman, should be in the hands and custody of his mother's kindred, sequestered in manner[4] from their company and attendance, of which every one ought[5] him as faithful service as they, and many of them far more honorable part of kin than his mother's side, "whose blood," quod[6] he, "saving the king's pleasure, was full unmeetly[7] to be matched with his; which now to be, as who say[8] removed from the king and the less noble to be left about him, is," quod he, "neither honorable to his majesty nor unto us, and also to his grace no surety to have the mightiest of his friends from him, and unto us no little jeopardy to suffer our well-proved evil willers to grow in overgreat authority with the prince in youth, namely which is light of belief[9] and soon persuaded.

"Ye remember, I trow,[1] King Edward himself, albeit he was

9. prudent.
1. Those charged with governance of the prince included Rivers, Hastings, John Alcock (Bishop of Worcester), Sir Thomas Vaughan, Sir Richard Hawte.
2. whereby . . . favor: i.e., the prince would favor those who had been his companions when he was a child.
3. revealed.   4. in manner: as it were.   5. owed.
6. said.   7. unsuitable.
8. as who say: as it were; "which" in the preceding clause refers to the young king's kindred on his father's side.
9. namely . . . belief: since it (youth) is credulous.   1. trust.

a man of age and of discretion, yet was he in many things ruled by the bend², more than stood either with his honor or our profit, or with the commodity³ of any man else, except only the immoderate advancement of themself. Which whether they sorer thirsted after their own weal⁴ or our woe, it were hard, I ween, to guess. And if some folks' friendship had not holden better place with the king than any respect of kindred, they might peradventure easily have betrapped and brought to confusion⁵ some of us ere this. Why not as easily as they have done some other already,⁶ as near of his royal blood as we? But our Lord hath wrought His will, and thank be to His grace that peril is past. Howbeit, as great is growing if we suffer this young king in our enemies' hand, which without his witting⁷ might abuse the name of his commandment to any of our undoing,⁸ which thing God and good provision⁹ forbid. Of which good provision none of us hath anything the less need for the late made atonement¹ in which the king's pleasure had more place than the parties' wills. Nor none of us, I believe, is so unwise oversoon to trust a new friend made of an old foe, or to think that an hoverly² kindness, suddenly contract³ in one hour, continued yet scant a fortnight, should be deeper settled in their stomachs than a long accustomed malice many years rooted."

With these words and writings and such other, the Duke of Gloucester soon set afire them that were of themself ethe⁴ to kindle, and in especial twain, Edward Duke of Buckingham⁵ and Richard⁶ Lord Hastings and chamberlain, both men of honor and of great power, the one by long succession from his

---

2. faction.   3. benefit.   4. well-being.   5. destruction.
6. *some other already:* i.e., the Duke of Clarence.
7. knowledge.   8. *to . . . undoing:* to the undoing of any of us.
9. foresight carefully exercised.
1. *for . . . atonement:* because of the recent agreement.
2. superficial.   3. contracted.   4. easy.
5. Actually *Henry*, second Duke of Buckingham (1454–83), who had been forced into a marriage with Elizabeth Woodville's sister Catherine in 1466.   6. i.e., William. See above, p. 11 and n. 7.

ancestry, the other by his office and the king's favor. These two, not bearing each to other so much love, as hatred both unto the queen's party, in this point accorded together with the Duke of Gloucester that they would utterly amove[7] fro the king's company all his mother's friends under the name of their enemies.

Upon this concluded, the Duke of Gloucester, understanding that the lords which at that time were about the king intended to bring him up to his coronation,[8] accompanied with such power of their friends that it should be hard for him to bring his purpose to pass without the gathering and great assemble[9] of people and in manner of open war, whereof the end he wist was doubtous,[1] and in which the king being on their side, his part should have the face and name of a rebellion, he secretly therefore by divers means caused the queen to be persuaded and brought in the mind that it neither were need and also should be jeopardous the king to come up strong. For whereas now every lord loved other and none other thing studied upon but about the coronation and honor of the king, if the lords of her kindred should assemble in the king's name much people, they should give the lords atwixt whom and them had been sometime debate, to fear and suspect, lest they should gather this people, not for the king's safeguard whom no man impugned, but for their destruction, having more regard to their old variance than their new atonement.[2] For which cause they should assemble on the other party much people again for their defense, whose power she wist well far stretched. And thus should all the realm fall on a roar.[3] And of all the hurt that thereof should ensue, which was likely not to be little, and the most harm there like to fall where she least would, all the world would put her and her kindred in the wight[4] and say that they had unwisely and untruly also, broken the amity and peace that

queen would be blamed

---

7. *utterly amove:* completely dismiss.
8. set by the Council for May 4, 1483.   9. assembling.
1. doubtful.   2. agreement.   3. *on a roar:* into confusion.
4. blame.

the king her husband so prudently made between his kin and hers in his deathbed and which the other party faithfully observed.

The queen, being in this wise persuaded, such word sent unto her son[5] and unto her brother,[6] being about the king; and over that the Duke of Gloucester himself and other lords, the chief of his bende,[7] wrote unto the king so reverently, and to the queen's friends there so lovingly, that they nothing earthly mistrusting, brought the king up in great haste, not in good speed,[8] with a sober[9] company.

Now was the king in his way to London gone from Northampton, when these Dukes of Gloucester and Buckingham came thither. Where remained behind the Lord Rivers, the king's uncle, intending on the morrow[1] to follow the king and be with him at Stony Stratford, eleven miles thence, early or[2] he departed. So was there made that night much friendly cheer between these dukes and the Lord Rivers a great while.

But incontinent[3] after that they were openly with great courtesy departed and the Lord Rivers lodged, the dukes secretly with a few of their most privy friends set them down in council, wherein they spent a great part of the night. And at their rising in the dawning of the day, they sent about privily to their servants in their inns and lodgings about, giving them commandment to make themself shortly[4] ready, for their lords were to horsebackward.[5] Upon which messages, many of their folk were attendant, when many of the Lord Rivers' servants were unready. Now had these dukes taken also into their custody the keys of the inn, that none should pass forth without their license. And over this, in the highway toward Stony Stratford

---

5. Richard Grey, the second son of Elizabeth Woodville by her first husband.

6. Anthony, Earl Rivers.   7. faction.

8. *in . . . speed:* at a normal rate of progress.

9. moderate in number.

1. Wednesday, April 30.   2. before.   3. immediately.

4. quickly.   5. *to horse backward:* ready to ride.

where the king lay, they had bestowed certain of their folk that should send back again and compel to return any man that were gotten out of Northampton toward Stony Stratford, till they should give other license; forasmuch as the dukes themself intended, for the show of their diligence, to be the first that should that day attend upon the king's highness out of that town —thus bare they folk in hand.[6]

But when the Lord Rivers understood the gates closed and the ways on every side beset, neither his servants nor himself suffered to gone[7] out, perceiving well so great a thing without his knowledge not begun for nought, comparing this manner present with this last night's cheer, in so few hours so great a change marvelously misliked. Howbeit sith[8] he could not get away—and keep himself close[9] he would not, lest he should seem to hide himself for some secret fear of his own fault, whereof he saw no such cause in himself—he determined upon the surety of his own conscience, to go boldly to them and inquire what this matter might mean. Whom, as soon as they saw, they began to quarrel with him and say that he intended to set distance between the king and them and to bring them to confusion, but it should not lie in his power. And when he began (as he was a very well spoken man) in goodly wise to excuse himself, they tarried not the end of his answer, but shortly took him and put him in ward,[1] and, that done, forthwith went to horseback and took the way to Stony Stratford, where they found the king with his company ready to leap on horseback and depart forward, to leave that lodging for them because it was too strait[2] for both companies.

And as soon as they came in his presence, they light adown[3] with all their company about them. To whom the Duke of Buckingham said, "Go afore, gentlemen and yeomen, keep your rooms."[4] And thus in a goodly array, they came to the king and

---

6. *bare . . . hand:* did they delude people.   7. go.   8. since.
9. confined.   1. *in ward:* under arrest.   2. small.
3. *light adown:* dismounted.   4. stations.

on their knees in very humble wise salved[5] his grace, which received them in very joyous and amiable manner, nothing earthly knowing nor mistrusting as yet. But even, by and by,[6] in his presence, they picked a quarrel to[7] the Lord Richard Grey, the king's other brother by his mother, saying that he, with the lord marquis[8] his brother and the Lord Rivers his uncle, had compassed[9] to rule the king and the realm, and to set variance among the states,[1] and to subdue and destroy the noble blood of the realm. Toward the accomplishing whereof, they said that the lord marquis had entered into the Tower of London, and thence taken out the king's treasure, and sent men to the sea.[2] All which thing these dukes wist well were done for good purposes and necessary by the whole council at London, saving that somewhat they must say. Unto which words the king answered, "What my brother marquis hath done I cannot say.[3] But, in good faith, I dare well answer for mine uncle Rivers and my brother here, that they be innocent of any such matters."

"Yea, my liege," quod the Duke of Buckingham, "they have kept their dealing in these matters far fro the knowledge of your good grace." And forthwith they arrested the Lord Richard and Sir Thomas Vaughan,[4] knight, in the king's presence, and brought the king and all back unto Northampton where they took again further counsel. And there they sent away from the king whom it pleased them, and set new servants about him, such as liked better them than him. At which dealing he wept and was nothing content, but it booted[5] not. And at dinner the Duke of Gloucester sent a dish from his own table to the Lord Rivers,

5. saluted.   6. *by and by:* at once.   7. with.
8. Dorset (Thomas Grey).   9. plotted.   1. noblemen.
2. Woodville's naval action was almost certainly a mere continuation of Edward IV's policy toward France.
3. Dorset was still in London and had not been with the Prince in Wales.
4. Sir Thomas Vaughan (d. 1483), a great Yorkist warrior, had been made chamberlain and councillor to Prince Edward in 1473.
5. availed.

praying him to be of good cheer, all should be well enough. And he thanked the duke, and prayed the messenger to bear it to his nephew, the Lord Richard, with the same message for his comfort, who he thought had more need for comfort, as one to whom such adversity was strange. But himself had been all his days in ure therewith,[6] and therefore could bear it the better. But for all this comfortable courtesy of the Duke of Gloucester, he sent the Lord Rivers and the Lord Richard with Sir Thomas Vaughan into the north country into divers places to prison, and afterward all to Pomfret, where they were in conclusion beheaded.[7]

In this wise the Duke of Gloucester took upon himself the order and governance of the young king, whom with much honor and humble reverence he conveyed upward toward the city. But anon the tidings of this matter came hastily to the queen, a little before the midnight following, and that in the sorest wise, that the king her son was taken; her brother, her son, and her other friends arrested and sent no man wist whither, to be done with God wot[8] what. With which tidings, the queen, in great flight[9] and heaviness, bewailing her child's ruin, her friends' mischance, and her own infortune,[1] damning the time that ever she dissuaded[2] the gathering of power about the king, gat[3] herself in all the haste possible with her younger son and her daughters out of the palace of Westminster, in which she then lay, into the sanctuary,[4] lodging herself and her company there in the abbot's[5] place.

Now came there one in likewise, not long after midnight, fro the lord chamberlain unto the Archbishop of York,[6] then

6. *in ure therewith:* used to it.
7. They were not executed until June 25, after the execution of Hastings.   8. knew.   9. fright.   1. ill fortune.
2. argued against.   3. got.
4. Located next to the palace at Westminster.
5. John Esteney, abbot from 1474–98.
6. Thomas Rotherham, alias Thomas Scot (1423–1500) Keeper of the Privy Seal (1467), Bishop of Rochester (1468) and Lincoln (1471), Archbishop of York (1480) and appointed Lord Chancellor by Edward in 1474. Though arrested on June 13, he was released on July 6.

Chancellor of England, to his place[7] not far from Westminster. And for that[8] he showed his servants that he had tidings of so great importance that his master gave him in charge not to forbear[9] his rest, they letted[1] not to wake him, nor he to admit this messenger into his bedside. Of whom he heard that these dukes were gone back with the king's grace from Stony Stratford unto Northampton. "Notwithstanding, sir," quod he, "my lord sendeth your lordship word that there is no fear, for he assureth you that all shall be well."

"I assure him," quod the archbishop, "be it as well as it will, it will never be so well as we have seen it." And thereupon, by and by,[2] after the messenger departed, he caused in all the haste all his servants to be called up, and so, with his own household about him, and every man weaponed, he took the great seal with him and came, yet before day, unto the queen. About whom he found much heaviness,[3] rumble, haste and business, carriage[4] and conveyance of her stuff into sanctuary—chests, coffers, packs, fardelles,[5] trusses,[6] all on men's backs, no man unoccupied, some lading,[7] some going, some discharging, some coming for more, some breaking down the walls to bring in the next[8] way, and some yet drew to[9] them that holp[1] to carry a wrong way. The queen herself sat alone alowe[2] on the rushes, all desolate and dismayed, whom the archbishop comforted in the best manner he could, showing her that he trusted the matter was nothing so sore as she took it for, and that he was put in good hope and out of fear by the message sent him from the lord chamberlain.

"Ah, woe worth him,"[3] quod she, "for he is one of them that laboreth to destroy me and my blood."

7. York Place, the residence of the Archbishop from the time of Walter Grey (d. 1225) until that of Wolsey (1529).
8. *for that:* because.   9. refrain from interrupting.   1. omitted.
2. *by and by:* soon.
3. grief.   4. carrying.   5. bundles.   6. packs.
7. loading.   8. shortest.   9. *drew to:* followed.   1. helped.
2. below.   3. *woe ... him:* may evil befall him.

"Madam," quod he, "be ye of good cheer. For I assure you if they crown any other king than your son whom they now have with them, we shall on the morrow crown his brother whom you have here with you. And here is the great seal, which in likewise as that noble prince, your husband, delivered it unto me, so here I deliver it unto you to the use and behoof of your son." And therewith he betook[4] her the great seal and departed home again, yet in the dawning of the day. By which time he might in his chamber window see all the Thames full of boats of the Duke of Gloucester's servants, watching that no man should go to sanctuary, nor none could pass unsearched.

Then was there great commotion and murmur as well in other places about, as specially in the city, the people diversely divining upon this dealing. And some lords, knights, and gentlemen, either for favor of the queen, or for fear of themself, assembled in sundry companies, and went flockmeal[5] in harness,[6] and many also for that they reckoned this demeanor[7] attempted not so specially against the other lords, as against the king himself in the disturbance of his coronation.

But then, by and by, the lords assembled together at London. Toward which meeting, the Archbishop of York, fearing that it would be ascribed (as it was indeed) to his overmuch lightness that he so suddenly had yielded up the great seal to the queen, to whom the custody thereof nothing pertained without especial commandment of the king, secretly sent for the seal again and brought it with him after the customable[8] manner. And at this meeting the Lord Hastings, whose truth[9] toward the king no man doubted nor needed to doubt, persuaded the lords to believe that the Duke of Gloucester was sure and fastly faithful to his prince and that the Lord Rivers and Lord Richard, with the other knights, were for matters attempted by them against the Dukes of Gloucester and Buckingham, put under arrest for their[1] surety, not for the king's jeopardy; and that they were

---

4. gave.   5. in groups.   6. armor.   7. business, action.
8. usual.   9. loyalty.   1. i.e., that of the dukes.

also in safeguard, and there no longer should remain than till the matter were, not by the dukes only, but also by all the other lords of the king's council indifferently[2] examined and by other discretions ordered, and either judged or appeased. But one thing he advised them beware, that they judged not the matter too far forth ere they knew the truth; nor turning their private grudges into the common hurt, irritating and provoking men unto anger, and disturbing the king's coronation, toward which the dukes were coming up, that they might peradventure bring the matter so far out of joint that it should never be brought in frame[3] again. Which strife, if it should hap, as it were likely, to come to a field,[4] though both parties were in all other things equal, yet should the authority be on that side where the king is himself.

With these persuasions of the Lord Hastings, whereof part himself believed, of part he wist[5] the contrary,[6] these commotions were somewhat appeased, but specially by that that[7] the Dukes of Gloucester and Buckingham were so near and came so shortly[8] on with the king, in none other manner, with none other voice or semblance, than to his coronation, causing the fame[9] to be blown about that these lords and knights which were taken had contrived the destruction of the Dukes of Gloucester and Buckingham, and of other the noble blood of the realm, to the end that themself would alone demean[1] and govern the king at their pleasure. And for the colorable[2] proof thereof, such of the dukes' servants as rode with the carts of their stuff that were taken (among which stuff no marvel though some were harness,[3] which at the breaking up of that household must needs either be brought away or cast away) they showed unto the people all the way as they went: "Lo, here be the barrels of harness that these traitors had privily conveyed

---

2. impartially.   3. *in frame:* into order.   4. battle.   5. knew.
6. Hasting's support of the duke at this time was primarily a matter of expediency. He trusted neither the Woodvilles nor Richard.
7. *by that that:* because.   8. quickly.   9. report.
1. rule.   2. feigned.   3. armor.

in their carriage to destroy the noble lords withal." This device, albeit that it made the matter to wise men more unlikely, well perceiving that the intenders of such a purpose would rather have had their harness on their backs than to have bound them up in barrels, yet much part of the common people were therewith very well satisfied and said it were almoise[4] to hang them.

When the king approached near to the city, Edmund Shaa,[5] goldsmith, then mayor, with William White and John Mathew, sheriffs, and all the other aldermen in scarlet, with five hundred horse of the citizens in violet, received him reverently at Hornsea, and riding from thence, accompanied him into the city, which he entered the fourth day of May, the first and last year of his reign. But the Duke of Gloucester bare him in open sight so reverently to the prince, with all semblance of lowliness,[6] that from the great obloquy in which he was so late before, he was suddenly fallen in so great trust, that at the council next assembled, he was made the only man chose[7] and thought most meet to be protector of the king and his realm, so that (were it destiny or were it folly) the lamb was betaken[8] to the wolf to keep. At which council also the Archbishop of York, Chancellor of England, which had delivered up the great seal to the queen, was thereof greatly reproved, and the seal taken from him and delivered to Doctor Russell,[9] Bishop of Lincoln, a wise man and a good and of much experience, and one of the best learned men undoubtedly that England had in his time. Divers lords and knights were appointed into divers rooms.[1] The lord chamberlain and some other[2] kept still their offices that they had before.

Now all were it so that the protector so sore thirsted for the

---

4. a good deed.
5. Edmund Shaa (d. 1487), Mayor of London in 1483.
6. humility.   7. chosen.   8. handed over.
9. John Russell (d. 1494) became Bishop of Lincoln in 1480. He was actually given the great seal on June 27, 1483, at Baynard's Castle.
1. offices.
2. Hastings and Thomas Stanley, Steward of the Household, retained their offices, at least temporarily.

finishing of that he had begun, that thought every day a year till it were achieved, yet durst he no further attempt as long as he had but half his prey in his hand, well witting that if he deposed the one brother, all the realm would fall to the other, if he either remained in sanctuary or should haply[3] be shortly conveyed to his farther liberty. Wherefore, incontinent[4] at the next meeting of the lords at the council, he proposed unto them that it was a heinous deed of the queen and proceeding of great malice toward the king's counsellors, that she should keep in sanctuary the king's brother from him, whose special pleasure and comfort were to have his brother with him. And that by her done to none other intent, but to bring all the lords in obloquy and murmur of the people, as though they were not to be trusted with the king's brother, that by the assent of the nobles of the land were appointed, as the king's nearest friends, to the tuition[5] of his own royal person. "The prosperity whereof standeth," quod he, "not all in keeping from enemies or ill viand,[6] but partly also in recreation and moderate pleasure, which he cannot, in this tender youth, take in the company of ancient[7] persons, but in the familiar conversation of those that be neither far under nor far above his age, and nevertheless of estate convenient[8] to accompany his noble majesty. Wherefore, with whom rather than with his own brother? And if any man think this consideration light (which I think no man thinketh that loveth the king) let him consider that sometime without small things, greater cannot stand. And verily it redoundeth greatly to the dishonor both of the king's highness and of all us that been about his grace, to have it run in every man's mouth, not in this realm only, but also in other lands (as evil words walk far) that the king's brother should be fain to keep sanctuary. For every man will ween that no man will so do for nought. And such evil opinion

---

3. perchance.   4. immediately.   5. guardianship.
6. *ill viand:* bad food or diet, possibly hinting at poison.
7. old, aged.   8. *estate convenient:* suitable rank in society.

once fastened in men's hearts, hard it is to wrest out, and may grow to more[9] grief than any man here can divine.

"Wherefore me thinketh it were not worst to send unto the queen for the redress of this matter some honorable, trusty man, such as both tendereth[1] the king's weal and the honor of his counsel, and is also in favor and credence with her. For all which considerations, none seemeth me more meetly[2] than our reverent father here present, my lord cardinal,[3] who may in this matter do most good of any man, if it please him to take the pain. Which I doubt not, of his goodness, he will not refuse, for the king's sake and ours, and wealth[4] of the young duke himself, the king's most honorable brother, and after my sovereign lord himself, my most dear nephew, considered that thereby shall be ceased the slanderous rumor and obloquy now going and the hurts avoided that thereof might ensue, and much rest and quiet grow to all the realm. And if she be percase[5] so obstinate and so precisely set upon her own will that neither his wise and faithful advertisement[6] can move her, nor any man's reason content her, then shall we, by mine advice, by the king's authority fetch him out of that prison and bring him to his noble presence, in whose continual company he shall be so well cherished and so honorably entreated[7] that all the world shall to our honor and her reproach perceive that it was only malice, frowardness,[8] or folly that caused her to keep him there. This is my mind in this matter for this time, except any of your lordships anything perceive to the contrary. For never shall I, by God's grace, so wed myself to mine own will, but that I shall be ready to change it upon your better advises." [9]

When the protector had said, all the council affirmed that the motion was good and reasonable, and to the king and the duke his brother honorable, and a thing that should cease great mur-

9. greater.   1. esteems.   2. fitting.
3. Thomas Bourchier (1404?–86) Archbishop of Canterbury from 1454 and Cardinal from 1467 until his death.   4. well-being.
5. by chance.   6. admonition.   7. treated.   8. perversity.
9. opinions.

mur in the realm, if the mother might be by good means induced
to deliver him. Which thing the Archbishop of York,[1] whom
they all agreed also to be thereto most convenient, took upon
him to move her, and therein to do his uttermost devoir.[2]
Howbeit if she could be in no wise entreated with her good
will to deliver him, then thought he and such other as were of
the spirituality present that it were not in any wise to be attempted to take him out against her will. For it would be a
thing that should turn to the great grudge of all men and high
displeasure of God if the privilege of that holy place should now
be broken, which had so many years been kept, which both
kings and popes so good had granted, so many had confirmed,
and which holy ground was more than five hundred year ago
by Saint Peter,[3] his own person in spirit, accompanied with
great multitude of angels, by night so specially hallowed and
dedicate to God (for the proof whereof they have yet in the
abbey Saint Peter's cope to show) that from that time hither-
ward was there never so undevout a king that durst that sacred
place violate, or so holy a bishop that durst it presume to consecrate. "And therefore," quod the Archbishop of York,[4] "God
forbid that any man should for anything earthly enterprise[5] to
break the immunity and liberty of that sacred sanctuary that
hath been the safeguard of so many a good man's life. And I
trust," quod he, "with God's grace, we shall not need it. But for
any manner need, I would not we should do it. I trust that she
shall be with reason contented, and all thing in good manner
obtained. And if it happen that I bring it not so to pass, yet shall
I toward it so far forth do my best, that ye shall all well perceive
that no lack of my devoir,[6] but the mother's dread and womanish fear shall be the let."[7]

1. An error for Canterbury.

2. *do . . . devoir:* make the greatest possible effort.

3. According to legend, in the early seventh century Edric, a fisher-
man, saw St. Peter consecrate the Abbey the night before the ceremony
was to have been performed by the first Bishop of London, Mellitus.

4. i.e., Canterbury.   5. attempt.   6. duty.   7. hindrance.

"Womanish fear, nay, womanish frowardness," quod the
Duke of Buckingham. "For I dare take it upon my soul, she well
knoweth she needeth no such thing to fear, either for her son
or for herself. For, as for her, here is no man that will be at war
with women. Would God some of the men of her kin were
women too, and then should all be soon in rest. Howbeit, there is
none of her kin the less loved for that they be her kin, but for
their own evil deserving. And nevertheless, if we loved neither
her nor her kin, yet were there no cause to think that we should
hate the king's noble brother, to whose grace we ourself be of
kin. Whose honor, if she as much desired as our dishonor, and
as much regard took to his wealth[8] as to her own will, she would
be as loath to suffer him from the king as any of us be. For if
she have any wit (as would God she had as good will as she hath
shrewd wit), she reckoneth herself no wiser than she thinketh
some that be here, of whose faithful mind she nothing doubteth,
but verily believeth and knoweth that they would be as sorry of
his harm as herself, and yet would have him from her if she
bide there. And we all, I think, content that both be with her, if
she come thence and bide in such place where they may with
their honor be.

"Now then, if she refuse in the deliverance of him, to follow
the counsel of them whose wisdom she knoweth, whose truth
she well trusteth, it is ethe[9] to perceive that frowardness letteth[1]
her, and not fear. But go to,[2] suppose that she fear (as who may
let her to fear her own shadow), the more she feareth to deliver
him, the more ought we fear to leave him in her hands. For if
she cast such fond[3] doubts that she fear his hurt, then will she
fear that he shall be fet[4] thence. For she will soon think that if
men were set (which God forbid) upon so great a mischief, the

---

8. well-being.
9. easy.
1. hinders (note the series of puns constructed around the word 'let'
and variants).
2. *go to:* come come.   3. foolish.   4. fetched.

sanctuary would little let them. Which good men might, as me thinketh, without sin somewhat less regard than they do.[5]

"Now then, if she doubt lest he might be fetched from her, is it not likely enough that she shall send him somewhere out of the realm? Verily, I look for none other. And I doubt not but she now as sore[6] mindeth it, as we the let[7] thereof. And if she might happen to bring that to pass (as it were no great maistry,[8] we letting her alone), all the world would say that we were a wise sort of counsellors about a king that let his brother be cast away under our noses. And therefore I ensure you faithfully for my mind, I will rather, maugry her mind,[9] fetch him away than leave him there, till her frowardness or fond fear convey him away. And yet will I break no sanctuary therefore. For verily, sith the privileges of that place and other like have been of long continued, I am not he that would be about to break them. And, in good faith, if they were now to begin, I would not be he that should be about to make them. Yet will I not say nay, but that it is a deed of pity that such men as the sea[1] or their evil debtors have brought in poverty should have some place of liberty to keep their bodies out of the danger of their cruel creditors. And also if the crown happen, as it hath done, to come in question, while either part taketh other as traitors, I will well there be some places of refuge for both. But as for thieves, of which these places be full, and which never fall fro the craft after they once fall thereto, it is pity the sanctuary should serve them. And much more mannequellers[2] whom God bade to take from the altar and kill them if their murder were willful.[3] And where it is otherwise there need we not the sanctuaries that God appointed in the old law.[4] For if either necessity, his own de-

5. The right of sanctuary was a serious political question in the late fifteenth and early sixteenth centuries.
6. eagerly.   7. hindrance.   8. achievement.
9. *maugry her mind:* despite her wish.
1. *such . . . sea:* i.e., merchants who have lost their goods through shipwreck.   2. murderers.   3. *Exodus* 21 : 14.
4. Cf. *Numbers* 35 : 22–31 which discusses places of refuge for those who commit accidental murder.

fense, or misfortune draw him to that deed, a pardon serveth which either the law granteth of course, or the king of pity may.

"Then look me[5] now how few sanctuary men there be whom any favorable necessity compelled to go thither. And then see on the other side what a sort there be commonly therein, of them whom willful unthriftiness hath brought to nought. What a rabble of thieves, murderers, and malicious, heinous traitors, and that in two places specially: the one[6] at the elbow of the city, the other in the very bowels.[7] I dare well avow it; weigh the good that they do with the hurt that cometh of them, and ye shall find it much better to lack both than have both. And this I say, although they were not abused as they now be and so long have been, that I fear me ever they will be while men be afeard[8] to set their hands to the mendment[9]—as though God and Saint Peter were the patrons of ungracious living.

"Now unthrifts[1] riot and run in debt upon the boldness of[2] these places; yea, and rich men run thither with poor men's goods—there they build, there they spend, and bid their creditors go whistle them.[3] Men's wives run thither with their husbands' plate,[4] and say they dare not abide with their husbands for beating. Thieves bring thither their stolen goods and there live thereon. There devise they new robberies; nightly they steal out; they rob and reve[5] and kill, and come in again as though those places gave them not only a safeguard for the harm they have done, but a license also to do more. Howbeit, much of this mischief, if wise men would set their hands to it, might be amended, with great thank of God and no breach of the privilege. The residue, sith so long ago I wot never what pope and what prince more piteous than politic[6] hath granted it and other

5. *look me:* notice.
6. *the one:* i.e., the sanctuary at Westminster itself.
7. The sanctuary of St. Martin Le Grand in the city came under the jurisdiction of Westminster Abbey in 1503.
8. afraid.   9. amendment.   1. spendthrifts.
2. *upon . . . of:* on the security of.
3. *go whistle them:* go and do what they will.
4. silver.   5. plunder.   6. prudent.

men since of a certain religious fear have not broken it, let us take a pain therewith and let it a God's name stand in force, as far forth as reason will. Which is not fully so far forth as may serve to let us of[7] the fetching forth of this noble man to his honor and wealth, out of that place in which he neither is nor can be a sanctuary man.

"A sanctuary serveth alway to defend the body of that man that standeth in danger abroad, not of great hurt only, but also of lawful hurt. For against unlawful harms, never pope nor king intended to privilege any one place. For that privilege hath every place. Knoweth any man any place wherein it is lawful one man to do another wrong? That no man unlawfully take hurt, that liberty, the king, the law, and very nature[8] forbiddeth in every place, and maketh to that regard[9] for every man every place a sanctuary. But where a man is by lawful means in peril, there needeth he the tuition[1] of some special privilege, which is the only ground and cause of all sanctuaries. From which necessity this noble prince is far, whose love to his king nature and kindred proveth, whose innocence to all the world his tender youth proveth. And so sanctuary, as for him, neither none he needeth, nor also none can have. Men come not to sanctuary as they come to baptism, to require it by their godfathers. He must ask it himself that must have it. And reason, sith no man hath cause to have it but whose conscience[2] of his own fault maketh him feign need to require[3] it. What will[4] then hath yonder babe? Which, and[5] if he had discretion to require it, if need were, I dare say would now be right angry with them that keep him there. And I would think without any scruple of conscience, without any breach of privilege, to be somewhat more homely[6] with them that be there sanctuary men indeed. For if one go to sanctuary with another man's goods,

7. *let us of:* keep us from.
8. *very nature:* nature itself.
9. *to that regard:* in that respect.   1. protection.
2. *whose conscience:* i.e., he whose awareness.
3. ask for.   4. cause.   5. even.   6. rough.

why should not the king, leaving his body at liberty, satisfy[7] the part of his goods even within the sanctuary? For neither king nor pope can give any place such a privilege that it shall discharge a man of his debts, being able to pay."

And with that divers of the clergy that were present, whether they said it for his pleasure or as they thought, agreed plainly that by the law of God and of the church the goods of a sanctuary man should be delivered in payment of his debts, and stolen goods to the owner, and only liberty reserved him to get his living with the labor of his hands.

"Verily," quod the duke, "I think you say very truth. And what if a man's wife will take sanctuary because she list[8] to run from her husband? I would ween if she can allege none other cause, he may lawfully, without any displeasure to Saint Peter, take her out of Saint Peter's church by the arm. And if nobody may be taken out of sanctuary that sayeth he will bide there, then if a child will take sanctuary because he feareth to go to school, his master must let him alone. And as simple as that sample[9] is, yet is there less reason in our case than in that. For therein, though it be a childish fear, yet is there at the leastwise some fear. And herein is there none at all. And verily I have often heard of sanctuary men. But I never heard erst[1] of sanctuary children. And therefore, as for the conclusion of my mind, who so may have deserved to need it, if they think it for their surety, let them keep it. But he can be no sanctuary man that neither hath wisdom to desire it nor malice to deserve it, whose life or liberty can by no lawful process stand in jeopardy. And he that taketh one out of sanctuary to do him good, I say plainly that he breaketh no sanctuary."

When the duke had done, the temporal men whole[2] and good part of the spiritual also, thinking none hurt earthly meant toward the young babe, condescended,[3] in effect, that if he were not delivered, he should be fetched. Howbeit, they thought it

---

7. make satisfaction with.   8. desires.
9. example.   1. before.   2. altogether.   3. agreed.

all best, in the avoiding of all manner of rumor, that the lord cardinal should first assay[4] to get him with her good will. And thereupon all the council came unto the Star Chamber at Westminster. And the lord cardinal, leaving the protector with the council in the Star Chamber, departed into the sanctuary to the queen, with divers other lords with him, were it for the respect of his honor, or that she should by presence of so many perceive that this errand was not one man's mind, or were it for that the protector intended not in this matter to trust any one man alone, or else that if she finally were determined to keep him, some of that company had haply secret instruction, incontinent, maugry her mind,[5] to take him and to leave her no respite to convey him,[6] which she was likely to mind[7] after this matter broken[8] to her, if her time would in any wise serve her.

When the queen and these lords were come together in presence, the lord cardinal showed unto her that it was thought unto the protector and unto the whole council that her keeping of the king's brother in that place was the thing which highly souned[9] not only to the great rumor[1] of the people and their obloquy, but also to the importable[2] grief and displeasure of the king's royal majesty. To whose grace it were as singular comfort to have his natural brother in company, as it was their both dishonor and all theirs and hers also to suffer him in sanctuary. As though the one brother stood in danger and peril of the other. And he showed her that the council therefore had sent him unto her to require her[3] the delivery of him, that he might be brought unto the king's presence at his liberty, out of that place which they reckoned as a prison. And there should he be demeaned[4] according to his estate. And she in this doing should both do great good to the realm, pleasure to the council and profit to

---

4. try.   5. *incontinent . . . mind:* immediately, despite her wish.

6. *convey him:* smuggle the boy out of the kingdom.

7. plan.   8. was revealed.

9. gave rise.   1. loud expression of disapproval.

2. unbearable.   3. *require her:* ask her for.   4. treated.

herself, succor to her friends that were in distress,[5] and over that (which he wist well she specially tendered[6]), not only great comfort and honor to the king, but also to the young duke himself, whose both great wealth it were to be together, as well for many greater causes, as also for their both disport and recreation; which thing the lord[7] esteemed not slight, though it seem light, well pondering that their youth without recreation and play cannot endure, nor any stranger for the convenience of their both ages and estates so meetly in that point for any of them as either of them for other.

"My lord," quod the queen, "I say not nay, but that it were very convenient that this gentleman whom ye require were in the company of the king, his brother. And in good faith me thinketh it were as great commodity to them both, as for yet a while, to be in the custody of their mother, the tender age considered of the elder of them both, but specially the younger, which besides his infancy, that also needeth good looking to, hath a while been so sore diseased with sickness and is so newly rather a little amended than well recovered that I dare put no person earthly in trust with his keeping but myself only, considering that there is, as physicians say and as we also find, double the peril in the recidivation[8] that was in the first sickness, with which disease, nature, being forelabored,[9] forewearied and weaked,[1] waxeth[2] the less able to bear out a new surfeit.[3] And albeit there might be founden other that would haply do their best unto him, yet is there none that either knoweth better how to order him than I that so long have kept him, or is more tenderly like to cherish him than his own mother that bare him."

"No man denieth, good madam," quod the cardinal, "but that your grace were of all folk most necessary about your

5. Undoubtedly a veiled threat, for Rivers, Grey, and Vaughan were now in prison.
6. valued.
7. Presumably Gloucester. Other early texts read "lords."
8. relapse.   9. worn out with labor.   1. weakened.
2. grows.   3. illness.

children, and so would all the council not only be content, but also glad that ye were, if it might stand with your pleasure, to be in such place as might stand with their honor. But if you appoint yourself[4] to tarry here, then think they yet more convenient that the Duke of York were with the king, honorably at his liberty, to the comfort of them both, than here as a sanctuary man to their both dishonor and obloquy; sith there is not alway so great necessity to have the child be with the mother, but that occasion may sometime be such that it should be more expedient to keep him elsewhere. Which in this well appeareth that at such time as your dearest son, then prince and now king, should for his honor and good order of the country keep household in Wales, far out of your company, your grace was well content therewith yourself."

"Not very well content," quod the queen. "And yet the case is not like, for the one was then in health, and the other is now sick. In which case I marvel greatly that my lord protector is so desirous to have him in his keeping, where if the child in his sickness miscarried by nature, yet might he run into slander and suspicion of fraud. And where they call it a thing so sore against my child's honor and theirs also that he bideth in this place, it is all their honors there to suffer him bide where no man doubteth he shall be best kept. And that is here, while I am here, which as yet intend not to come forth and jeopard[5] myself after[6] other of my friends, which would God were rather here in surety with me than I were there in jeopardy with them."

"Why, madam," quod another lord,[7] "know you anything why they should be in jeopardy!"

"Nay, verily, sir," quod she, "nor why they should be in prison neither, as they now be. But it is, I trow,[8] no great marvel though[9] I fear, lest those that have not letted[1] to put them in

4. *appoint yourself:* resolve.   5. endanger.   6. like.
7. Perhaps John Howard, Duke of Norfolk, to whom this sentence is attributed in other early texts of the *History*.
8. believe.   9. that.   1. hesitated.

duress[2] without color,[3] will let as little to procure their destruction without cause."

The cardinal made a countenance to the other lord that he should harp no more upon that string. And then said he to the queen that he nothing doubted but that those lords of her honorable kin, which as yet remained under arrest, should, upon the matter examined, do well enough. And as toward her noble person, neither was nor could be, any manner jeopardy.

"Whereby should I trust that," quod the queen, "in that I am guiltless? As though they were guilty. In that I am with their enemies better beloved than they? When they hate them for my sake. In that I am so near of kin to the king? And how far be they off[4]—if that would help, as God send grace it hurt not. And therefore, as for me, I purpose not as yet to depart hence. And as for this gentleman, my son, I mind[5] that he shall be where I am till I see further. For I assure you, for that I see some men so greedy without any substantial cause to have him, this maketh me much the more farder[6] to deliver him."

"Truly, madam," quod he, "and the farder that you be to deliver him, the farder be other men to suffer you to keep him, lest your causeless fear might cause you farther to convey him. And many be there that think that he can have no privilege in this place, which neither can have will to ask it nor malice to deserve it. And therefore they reckon no privilege broken, though they fetch him out. Which, if ye finally refuse to deliver him, I verily think they will—so much dread hath my lord, his uncle, for the tender love he beareth him, lest your grace should hap to send him away."

"Ah, sir," quod the queen, "hath the protector so tender zeal to him that he feareth nothing but lest he should escape him? Thinketh he that I would send him hence, which neither is in the plight[7] to send out; and in what place could I reckon him sure, if he be not sure in this, the sanctuary whereof was

2. confinement.   3. allegeable excuse.   4. distant in kinship.
5. intend.   6. afraid.   7. condition.

there never tyrant yet so devilish that durst presume to break? And, I trust God, the most holy Saint Peter, the guardian of this sanctuary, is as strong now to withstand his adversaries as ever he was. But my son can deserve no sanctuary, and therefore he cannot have it. Forsooth, he hath found a goodly gloss[8] by which that place that may defend a thief may not save an innocent. 'But he is in no jeopardy nor hath no need thereof.' Would God he had not. Troweth the protector (I pray God he may prove a protector), troweth he that I perceive not whereunto his painted process[9] draweth? 'It is not honorable that the duke bide here; it were comfortable for them both that he were with his brother because the king lacketh a play fellow'—be ye sure. I pray God send them both better play fellows than him that maketh so high a matter upon such a trifling pretext, as though there could none be founden to play with the king but if[1] his brother that hath no lust to play, for sickness, come out of sanctuary, out of his safeguard, to play with him. As though princes, as young as they be, could not play but with their peers, or children could not play but with their kindred, with whom, for the more part, they agree much worse than with strangers. 'But the child cannot require the privilege'—who told him so? He shall hear him ask it, and[2] he will. Howbeit this is a gay[3] matter. Suppose he could not ask it; suppose he would not ask it; suppose he would ask to go out: if I say he shall not, if I ask the privilege but for myself, I say he that against my will taketh out him breaketh the sanctuary. Serveth this liberty for my person only, or for my goods too? Ye may not hence take my horse fro me; and may you take my child fro me? He is also my ward; for, as my learned counsel showeth me, sith he hath nothing by descent holden by knight's service,[4] the law maketh his mother his guardian. Then may no man, I suppose, take my ward fro me

---

8. *goodly gloss:* plausible pretext.
9. *painted process:* feigned procedure.
1. *but if:* unless.   2. if.   3. immaterial.
4. *sith . . . service:* i.e., since he holds no land.

out of sanctuary without the breach of the sanctuary. And if my privilege could not serve him, nor he ask it for himself, yet sith the law committeth to me the custody of him, I may require it for him; except[5] the law give a child a guardian only for his goods and his lands, discharging him of the cure[6] and safe keeping of his body, for which only both lands and goods serve.

"And if examples be sufficient to obtain privilege for my child, I need not far to seek. For in this place in which we now be (and which is now in question whether my child may take benefit of it) mine other son, now king, was born and kept in his cradle and preserved to a more prosperous fortune, which I pray God long to continue. And as all you know, this is not the first time that I have taken sanctuary; for when my lord, my husband, was banished and thrust out of his kingdom, I fled hither being great with child, and here I bare the prince.[7] And when my lord, my husband, returned safe again and had the victory,[8] then went I hence to welcome him home; and from hence I brought my babe, the prince, unto his father, when he first took him in his arms. And I pray God that my son's palace may be as great safeguard to him now reigning, as this place was sometime to the king's enemy. In which place I intend to keep his brother since man's law serveth the guardian to keep the infant. The law of nature wills the mother keep her child. God's law privilegeth the sanctuary, and the sanctuary my son, sith I fear to put him in the protector's hands that hath his brother already, and were, if both failed, inheritor to the crown. The cause of my fear hath no man to do to examine. And yet fear I no further than the law feareth, which, as learned men tell me, forbiddeth every man the custody of them by whose

5. unless.   6. care.

7. Elizabeth took sanctuary at Westminster on October 1, 1470, when Edward IV was forced to flee from the country by Warwick. Edward V was born there on November 2.

8. i.e., won the Battle of Barnet, April 14, 1471. But Edward had actually joined his wife earlier, on April 11.

death he may inherit less land than a kingdom.[9] I can[1] no more, but whosoever he be that breaketh this holy sanctuary, I pray God shortly send him need of sanctuary when he may not come to it. For taken out of sanctuary would I not my mortal enemy were."

The lord cardinal, perceiving that the queen waxed ever the longer the further off and also that she began to kindle and chafe and speak sore, biting words against the protector, and such as he neither believed and was also loath to hear, he said unto her for a final conclusion that he would no longer dispute the matter. But if she were content to deliver the duke to him and to the other lords there present, he durst lay his own body and soul both in pledge, not only for his surety, but also for his estate.[2] And if she would give them a resolute answer to the contrary, he would forthwith depart therewithal, and shift[3] whoso would with this business afterward; for he never intended more to move her in that matter in which she thought that he and all other also, save herself, lacked either wit or truth—wit, if they were so dull that they could nothing perceive what the protector intended; truth, if they should procure her son to be delivered into his hands, in whom they should perceive toward the child any evil intended.

The queen with these words stood a good while in a great study. And forasmuch her seemed the cardinal more ready to depart than some of the remnant, and the protector himself ready at hand, so that she verily thought she could not keep him there, but that he should incontinent[4] be taken thence; and to convey him elsewhere neither had she time to serve her, nor place determined, nor persons appointed, all thing unready—this message came on her so suddenly—nothing less looking for than to have him fet[5] out of sanctuary, which she thought to be now beset in such places about that he could not be conveyed out untaken, and partly as she thought it might fortune her

9. *less . . . kingdom:* i.e., *even* less land than a kingdom.   1. know.
2. dignity.   3. deal.   4. soon.   5. fetched.

fear to be false,[6] so well she waste[7] it was either needless or boot-
less; wherefore, if she should needs go from him, she dempte[8] it
best to deliver him. And over that, of the cardinal's faith she
nothing doubted, nor of some other lords neither, whom she
there saw, which as she feared lest they might be deceived, so
was she well assured they would not be corrupted. Then
thought she it should yet make them the more warily to look to
him and the more circumspectly to see to his surety, if she with
her own hands betook him to them of trust.

And at the last she took the young duke by the hand and said
unto the lords: "My lord," quod she, "and all my lords, I
neither am so unwise to mistrust your wits nor so suspicious to
mistrust your troths.[9] Of which thing I purpose to make you
such a proof as, if either of both lacked in you, might turn
both me to great sorrow, the realm to much harm, and you to
great reproach. For, lo, here is," quod she, "this gentleman
whom I doubt not but I could here keep safe if I would, whatsoever any man say. And I doubt not also but there be some
abroad, so deadly enemies unto my blood that if they wist[1]
where any of it lay in their own body, they would let it out. We
have also had experience that the desire of a kingdom knoweth
no kindred. The brother hath been the brother's bane. And may
the nephews be sure of their uncle? Each of these children is
other's defense while they be asunder, and each of their lives
lieth in the other's body. Keep one safe and both be sure, and
nothing for them both more perilous than to be both in one
place. For what wise merchant adventureth all his good[2] in one
ship? All this notwithstanding, here I deliver him, and his
brother in him, to keep into your hands, of whom I shall ask
them both afore God and the world. Faithful ye be, that wot I
well, and I know well you be wise. Power and strength to keep
him, if ye list,[3] neither lack ye of yourself, nor can lack help in

6. *fortune . . . false:* happen that her fear was unjustified.
7. knew.   8. judged.   9. loyalty.   1. knew.
2. merchandise.   3. please.

this cause. And if ye cannot elsewhere, then may you leave him here. But only one thing I beseech you, for the trust that his father put in you ever and for the trust that I put in you now, that as far as ye think that I fear too much, be you well ware that you fear not as far too little."

And therewithal she said unto the child: "Farewell, my own sweet son; God send you good keeping. Let me kiss you once yet ere you go, for God knoweth when we shall kiss together again." And therewith she kissed him and blessed him, turned her back and wept and went her way, leaving the child weeping as fast.[4]

When the lord cardinal and these other lords with him had received this young duke, they brought him into the Star Chamber where the protector took him in his arms and kissed him with these words: "Now welcome, my lord, even with all my very heart." And he said in that of likelihood as he thought. Thereupon, forthwith, they brought him to the king, his brother, into the bishop's[5] palace at Paul's, and from thence through the city honorably into the Tower, out of which after that day they never came abroad.

When the protector had both the children in his hands, he opened himself more boldly, both to certain other men, and also chiefly to the Duke of Buckingham, although I know that many thought that this duke was privy to all the protector's counsel even from the beginning. And some of the protector's friends said that the duke was the first mover of the protector to this matter, sending a privy messenger unto him, straight after King Edward's death. But other again, which knew better the subtle wit of the protector, deny that he ever opened his enterprise to the duke until he had brought to pass the things before rehearsed.[6] But when he had imprisoned the queen's kinsfolks and gotten both her sons into his own hands, then he opened the rest of his purpose with less fear to them whom he

4. The prince was delivered from sanctuary on June 16.
5. Thomas Kemp, Bishop of London (c. 1414–89).   6. related.

thought meet for the matter, and specially to the duke, who being won to his purpose, he thought his strength more than half increased.

The matter was broken unto the duke by subtle folks and such as were their craft masters[7] in the handling of such wicked devises,[8] who declared unto him that the young king was offended with him for his kinsfolks' sakes, and that if he were ever able, he would revenge them, who would prick him forward[9] thereunto, if they escaped (for they would remember their imprisonment). Or else if they were put to death, without doubt the young king would be careful[1] for their deaths, whose imprisonment was grievous unto him. And that with repenting the duke should nothing avail, for there was no way left to redeem his offense by benefits, but he should sooner destroy himself than save the king, who with his brother and his kinsfolk he saw in such places imprisoned, as the protector might with a beck[2] destroy them all; and that it were no doubt but he would do it indeed, if there were any new enterprise attempted. And that it was likely that as the protector had provided privy guard for himself, so had he spialles[3] for the duke and trains[4] to catch him if he should be against him, and that, peradventure, from them whom he least suspected. For the state of things and the dispositions of men were then such that a man could not well tell whom he might trust or whom he might fear. These things and such like, being beaten into the duke's mind, brought him to that point that where he had repented the way that he had entered, yet would he go forth in the same; and since he had once begun, he would stoutly go through. And therefore to this wicked enterprise which he believed could not be voided,[5] he bent[6] himself and went through, and determined that since the common mischief could not be amended, he would turn it as much as he might to his own commodity.[7]

7. *their craft masters:* masters of the art.
8. plots.   9. *prick him forward:* provoke him.
1. deeply affected (with grief).   2. nod.   3. spies.   4. traps.
5. frustrated.   6. applied.   7. advantage.

Then it was agreed that the protector should have the duke's aid to make him king and that the protector's only lawful son[8] should marry the duke's daughter and that the protector should grant him the quiet possession of the Earldom of Hereford, which he claimed as his inheritance and could never obtain it in King Edward's time. Besides these requests of the duke, the protector of his own mind promised him a great quantity of the king's treasure and of his household stuff. And when they were thus at a point[9] between themselves, they went about to prepare for the coronation of the young king, as they would have it seem. And that they might turn both the eyes and minds of men from perceiving of their drifts[1] otherwise, the lords, being sent for from all parts of the realm, came thick to that solemnity. But the protector and the duke, after that, that they had set the lord cardinal, the Archbishop of York (then lord chancellor), the Bishop of Ely,[2] the Lord Stanley,[3] and the Lord Hastings (then lord chamberlain), with many other noble men to commune and devise about[4] the coronation in one place, as fast were they in another place contriving the contrary, and to make the protector king. To which council, albeit there were adhibit[5] very few and they very secret, yet began there, here and there about, some manner of muttering among the people, as though all should not long be well, though they neither wist what they feared nor wherefore; were it that before such great things, men's hearts of a secret instinct of nature misgiveth them, as

8. Edward (1473–84), Earl of Salisbury (1478) and Duke of Cornwall (1483), the only child of Richard and Anne Neville. Though Buckingham had two daughters, there is no record of this projected marriage in other accounts.

9. *at a point:* agreed.   1. plots.

2. John Morton (1420–1500) became Bishop of Ely in 1479. He succeeded Bourchier as Archbishop of Canterbury (1486), became Chancellor (1487) and was made a Cardinal (1493).

3. Thomas Stanley (1435–1504) first Earl of Derby (1485), a man of ambivalent political persuasion, married Margaret Beaufort, the mother of Henry VII, in 1482.

4. *devise about:* make plans with regard to.   5. admitted.

the sea without wind swelleth of himself sometime before a
tempest, or were it that some one man haply somewhat perceiving, filled many men with suspicion, though he showed few
men what he knew. Howbeit, somewhat the dealing self[6] made
men to muse on the matter, though the council were close.[7] For
little and little all folk withdrew from the Tower and drew to
Crosby's place in Bishopsgate Street where the protector kept
his household. The protector had the resort,[8] the king, in manner
desolate.[9] While some for their business made suit to them that
had the doing, some were by their friends secretly warned that
it might haply[1] turn them to no good to be too much attendant
about the king without the protector's appointment, which removed also divers of the prince's old servants from him and set
new about him.

Thus, many things coming together, partly by chance, partly
of purpose, caused, at length, not common people only, that
wave with the wind, but wise men also and some lords eke[2] to
mark the matter and muse thereon, so far forth that the Lord
Stanley, that was after Earl of Derby, wisely mistrusted it and
said unto the Lord Hastings that he much misliked these two
several councils.

"For while we," quod he, "talk of one matter in the one place,
little wot[3] we whereof they talk in the other place."

"My lord," quod the Lord Hastings, "on my life, never doubt
you. For while one man is there which is never thence, never can
there be thing once minded[4] that should sound[5] amiss toward
me, but it should be in mine ears ere it were well out of their
mouths."

This meant he by[6] Catesby,[7] which was of his near secret
counsel and whom he very familiarly used, and in his most
weighty matters put no man in so special trust, reckoning him-

---

6. itself.   7. secret.   8. assemblage of people.
9. *in . . . desolate:* as it were, solitary.   1. perchance.   2. too.
3. know.   4. planned.   5. appear.   6. concerning.
7. William Catesby (c. 1450–85), a trained lawyer, managed Hastings' estates.

self to no man so lief,[8] sith he well wist there was no man to him so much beholden as was this Catesby, which was a man well learned in the laws of this land, and by the special favor of the lord chamberlain, in good authority, and much rule bare in all the county of Leicester where the lord chamberlain's power chiefly lay. But surely great pity was it that he had not had either more truth or less wit. For his dissimulation only,[9] kept all that mischief up. In whom if the Lord Hastings had not put so special trust, the Lord Stanley and he had departed with divers other lords and broken all the dance,[1] for many ill signs that he saw, which he now construed all to the best: so surely thought he that there could be none harm toward him in that council intended where Catesby was.

And of truth the protector and the Duke of Buckingham made very good semblance unto the Lord Hastings and kept him much in company. And undoubtedly the protector loved him well and loath was to have lost him, saving for fear lest his life should have quailed[2] their purpose. For which cause he moved Catesby to prove with some words cast out afar off, whether he could think it possible to win the Lord Hastings into their part. But Catesby, whether he assayed him or assayed him not,[3] reported unto them that he found him so fast[4] and heard him speak so terrible words that he durst no further break.[5] And of truth the lord chamberlain of very trust showed unto Catesby the mistrust that other began to have in the matter. And therefore he, fearing lest their motions[6] might with the Lord Hastings minish his credence,[7] whereunto only all the matter leaned,[8] procured[9] the protector hastily to rid[1] him. And

---

8. beloved. 9. alone. 1. game. 2. impaired.

3. *whether . . . not:* whether or not he tested him. Catesby appears to have failed deliberately in his task of winning Hastings to Richard's side, thus committing double treason.

4. steadfast.

5. *durst . . . break:* dared not proceed any further with him.

6. propositions. 7. *minish his credence:* lessen his credit.

8. tended. 9. persuaded. 1. get rid of.

much the rather, for that he trusted by his death to obtain much of the rule that the Lord Hastings bare in his country, the only desire whereof[2] was the allective[3] that induced him to be partner and one special contriver of all this horrible treason.

Whereupon soon after, that is to wit, on the Friday, the thirteenth day of June, many lords assembled in the Tower and there sat in council, devising the honorable solemnity of the king's coronation, of which the time appointed then so near approached that the pageants and subtleties[4] were in making day and night at Westminster, and much victual killed therefor that afterward was cast away. These lords so sitting together comoning[5] of this matter, the protector came in among them, first about nine of the clock, saluting them courteously, and excusing himself that he had been from them so long, saying merrily that he had been asleep that day. And after a little talking with them, he said unto the Bishop of Ely: "My lord, you have very good strawberries at your garden in Holborn; I require you, let us have a mess of them."

"Gladly, my lord," quod he, "would God I had some better thing as ready to your pleasure as that." And therewith in all the haste he sent his servant for a mess of strawberries. The protector set the lords fast in comoning, and thereupon, praying them to spare him for a little while, departed thence.

And soon, after one hour, between ten and eleven, he returned into the chamber among them, all changed with a wonderful sour, angry countenance, knitting the brows, frowning and frothing and gnawing on his lips, and so sat him down in his place, all the lords much dismayed and sore marvelling of this manner of sudden change, and what thing should him ail. Then when he had sitten still awhile, thus he began: "What were they worthy to have that compass[6] and imagine the destruction

---

2. *the ... whereof:* and this desire alone.   3. enticement.
4. Probably symbolic figures which were to be placed on the banqueting tables.
5. talking.   6. plot.

of me, being so near of blood unto the king and protector of his
royal person and his realm?"

At this question all the lords sat sore astonied,[7] musing
much by whom this question should be meant, of which every
man wist himself clear. Then the lord chamberlain, as he that
for the love between them thought he might be boldest with
him, answered and said that they were worthy to be punished
as heinous traitors, whatsoever they were. And all the other
affirmed the same.

"That is," quod he, "yonder sorceress, my brother's wife, and
other with her"—meaning the queen.[8]

At these words, many of the other lords were greatly abashed
that favored her. But the Lord Hastings was in his mind better
content that it was moved by[9] her than any other whom he
loved better, albeit his heart somewhat grudged that he was not
afore made of counsel in this matter, as he was of the taking of
her kindred and of their putting to death, which were by his
assent before devised to be beheaded at Pomfret this selfsame
day,[1] in which he was not ware[2] that it was by other devised
that himself should the same day be beheaded at London.

Then said the protector: "Ye shall all see in what wise that
sorceress and that other witch of her counsel, Shore's wife,[3]
with their affinity,[4] have by their sorcery and witchcraft wasted
my body." And therewith he plucked up his doublet sleeve to
his elbow upon his left arm, where he showed a werish,[5] withered
arm and small (as it was never other). And thereupon every

7. *sore astonied:* completely dumbfounded.
8. Richard's accusation may have been prompted by a similar charge
(of witchcraft) brought against the queen's mother at the time of
Elizabeth's royal marriage.
9. *moved by:* said concerning.
1. *selfsame day:* in reality, not until June 25.   2. aware.
3. Jane Shore (c. 1440–1527?) née Lambert, wife of William Shore
(a wealthy mercer), became Edward IV's mistress about 1475; she
was kept by Hastings after the king's death, but apparently soon passed
to Dorset.
4. comrades.   5. shrivelled.

man's mind sore misgave them, well perceiving that this matter was but a quarrel, for well they wist that the queen was too wise to go about any such folly. And also, if she would, yet would she, of all folk, least make Shore's wife of counsel, whom of all women she most hated, as that concubine whom the king, her husband, had most loved. And also no man was there present but well knew that his arm was ever such since his birth.

Nevertheless the lord chamberlain (which fro the death of King Edward kept Shore's wife, on whom he somewhat doted in the king's life, saving, as it is said, he that while[6] forbare her of reverence toward his king, or else of a certain kind of fidelity to his friend) answered and said: "Certainly, my lord, if they have so heinously done, they be worthy heinous punishment."

"What!" quod the protector. "Thou servest me, I ween,[7] with 'ifs' and with 'ands.' I tell thee they have so done, and that I will make good on thy body, traitor."

And therewith, as in a great anger, he clapped his fist upon the board a great rap. At which token[8] given, one cried treason without the chamber. Therewith a door clapped, and in come there rushing men in harness,[9] as many as the chamber might hold. And anon the protector said to the Lord Hastings: "I arrest thee, traitor."

"What me, my lord?" quod he.

"Yea, thee, traitor," quod the protector.

And another[1] let fly at the Lord Stanley, which shrunk at the stroke and fell under the table, or else his head had been cleft to the teeth, for as shortly[2] as he shrank, yet ran the blood about his ears. Then were they all quickly bestowed in divers chambers except the lord chamberlain, whom the protector bade speed and shrive him apace;[3] "for by Saint Paul," quod he, "I will not to dinner till I see thy head off." It booted him not to ask why,

6. *that while:* during that time.   7. think.   8. signal.
9. armor.
1. Perhaps Richard Middleton (1430–87), one of Gloucester's supporters who is named in the Latin text.
2. quickly.   3. *shrive . . . apace:* go to confession at once.

but heavily[4] he took a priest at adventure[5] and made a short shrift, for a longer would not be suffered; the protector made so much haste to dinner, which he might not go to till this were done, for saving of his oath. So was he brought forth into the green beside the chapel within the Tower, and his head laid down upon a long log of timber, and there stricken off, and afterward his body with the head interred at Windsor beside the body of King Edward, whose both souls our Lord pardon.

A marvelous case is it to hear either the warnings of that he should have voided[6] or the tokens[7] of that he could not void. For the self[8] night next before his death, the Lord Stanley sent a trusty secret messenger unto him at midnight, in all the haste, requiring him to rise and ride away with him, for he was disposed utterly no longer to bide; he had so fearful a dream, in which him thought that a boar with his tusks so raced[9] them both by the heads that the blood ran about both their shoulders. And forasmuch as the protector gave the boar for his cognisaunce,[1] this dream made so fearful an impression in his heart that he was thoroughly determined no longer to tarry, but had his horse ready, if the Lord Hastings would go with him to ride so far yet the same night, that they should be out of danger ere day.

"Ay, good lord," quod the Lord Hastings to this messenger, "leaneth my lord, thy master, so much to such trifles and hath such faith in dreams, which either his own fear fantasieth or do rise in the night's rest by reason of his day thoughts? Tell him it is plain witchcraft to believe in such dreams, which, if they were tokens of things to come, why thinketh he not that we might be as likely to make them true by our going, if we were caught and brought back (as friends fail fleers[2]), for then had the boar a cause likely to race us with his tusks, as folk that fled for some falsehood; wherefore either is there no peril (nor none is there indeed), or if any be, it is rather in going than biding. And if

4. sadly.   5. random.   6. avoided.   7. portents.   8. very.
9. slashed.   1. coat of arms.   2. those who flee.

we should needs cost[3] fall in peril one way or other, yet had I
lever[4] that men should see it were by other men's falsehood than
think it were either our own fault or faint heart. And therefore
go to thy master, man, and commend me to him, and pray him
be merry and have no fear, for I ensure[5] him I am as sure of the
man that he woteth[6] of as I am of my own hand."

"God send grace, sir," quod the messenger, and went his way.

Certain is it also that in the riding toward the Tower the same
morning in which he was beheaded, his horse twice or thrice
stumbled with him almost to the falling, which thing, albeit
each man wot well daily happeneth to them to whom no such
mischance is toward,[7] yet hath it been of an old rite and custom
observed as a token oftentimes notably foregoing some great
misfortune. Now this that followeth was no warning, but an
enemious[8] scorn. The same morning, ere[9] he were up, came a
knight[1] unto him, as it were of courtesy, to accompany him to
the council, but of truth sent by the protector to haste him
thitherward, with whom he was of secret confederacy in that
purpose, a mean[2] man at that time, and now of great authority.
This knight, when it happed[3] the lord chamberlain by the way
to stay his horse and comen[4] awhile with a priest whom he met
in the Tower Street, brake his tale[5] and said merrily to him:
"What, my lord, I pray you, come on; whereto talk you so long
with that priest? You have no need of a priest yet." And therewith he laughed upon him, as though he would say, "ye shall
have soon." But so little wist the other what he meant, and so
little mistrusted, that he was never merrier nor never so full of
good hope in his life, which self thing is often seen a sign of

3. *needs cost:* necessarily.   4. rather.
5. assure.   6. knows.   7. approaching.
8. hostile, caused by his enemies.   9. before.
1. Probably Thomas Howard, second Duke of Norfolk (d. 1524), who
is named in the Harding-Hall versions of the text.
2. of low rank.   3. chanced.   4. converse.
5. *brake his tale:* interrupted his conversation.

change. But I shall rather let anything pass me[6] than the vain
surety of man's mind so near his death.

Upon the very Tower wharf, so near the place where his head
was off so soon after, there met he with one Hastings, a pursuivant[7] of his own name. And of their meeting in that place, he
was put in remembrance of another time, in which it had
happened them before to meet in like manner together in the
same place. At which other time the lord chamberlain had
been accused[8] unto King Edward by the Lord Rivers, the
queen's brother, in such wise that he was for the while (but it
lasted not long) far fallen into the king's indignation, and stood
in great fear of himself. And forasmuch as he now met this
pursuivant in the same place—that jeopardy so well passed—it
gave him great pleasure to talk with him thereof, with whom
he had before talked thereof in the same place while he was
therein.

And therefore he said, "Ah, Hastings, art thou remembered[9]
when I met thee here once with an heavy heart?"

"Yea, my lord," quod he, "that remember I well; and thanked
be God they gat[1] no good, nor ye none harm thereby."

"Thou wouldest say so," quod he, "if thou knewest as much
as I know, which few know else as yet and more shall shortly."
That meant he by[2] the lords of the queen's kindred that were
taken before and should that day be beheaded at Pomfret; which
he well wist, but nothing ware[3] that the axe hang over his own
head "In faith, man," quod he, "I was never so sorry,[4] nor
never stood in so great dread in my life as I did when thou and
I met here. And lo how the world is turned: now stand mine
enemies in the danger (as thou mayest hap to hear more here-

6. *pass me:* go unnoted.   7. royal messenger.
8. Apparently alluding to the incident described earlier, above, p. 11
(*CW 2,* 11/1–8). But Hastings was never out of favor with Edward IV
for very long.
9. *art . . . remembered:* Do you remember?   1. got.
2. *That . . . by:* He alluded to.   3. aware.   4. distressed.

after) and I never in my life so merry, nor never in so great surety."

O good God, the blindness of our mortal nature! When he most feared, he was in good surety; when he reckoned himself surest, he lost his life, and that within two hours after. Thus ended this honorable man, a good knight and a gentle, of great authority with his prince, of living somewhat desolate,[5] plain and open to his enemy and secret to his friend, eth[6] to beguile, as he that of good heart and courage[7] forestudied[8] no perils; a loving man and passing well beloved; very faithful and trusty enough, trusting too much.

Now flew the fame of this lord's death swiftly through the city, and so forth further about like a wind in every man's ear. But the protector immediately after dinner, intending to set some color upon[9] the matter, sent in all the haste for many substantial men out of the city into the Tower. And at their coming, himself, with the Duke of Buckingham, stood harnessed[1] in old ill-faring briginders,[2] such as no man should ween that they would vouchsafe to have put upon their backs, except that some sudden necessity had constrained them. And then the protector showed them that the lord chamberlain and other of his conspiracy had contrived to have suddenly destroyed him and the duke there, the same day, in the council. And what they intended further was as yet not well known. Of which their treason he never had knowledge before ten of the clock the same forenoon. Which sudden fear drove them to put on for their defense such harness as came next to hand. And so had God holpen[3] them that the mischief turned upon them that would have done it. And this he required them to report.

Every man answerd him fair,[4] as though no man mistrusted the matter, which of truth no man believed. Yet, for the further appeasing of the people's mind, he sent immediately after

5. dissolute.   6. easy.   7. disposition.   8. anticipated.
9. set . . . upon: give some pretext for   1. armored.
2. ill-faring briginders: poorly conditioned body arms for foot-soldiers.
3. helped.   4. civilly.

dinner, in all the haste, one herald of arms, with a proclamation to be made through the city in the king's name, containing that the Lord Hastings, with divers other of his traitorous purpose, had before conspired the same day to have slain the lord protector and the Duke of Buckingham, sitting in the council, and after to have taken upon them to rule the king and the realm at their pleasure, and thereby to pill and spoil[5] whom they list,[6] uncontrolled. And much matter was there in the proclamation devised to the slander of the lord chamberlain, as that he was an evil counsellor to the king's father, enticing him to many things highly redounding to the minishing of his honor and to the universal hurt of his realm, by his evil company, sinister procuring, and ungracious example, as well in many other things as in the vicious living and inordinate abusion[7] of his body, both with many other, and also specially with Shore's wife, which was one also of his most secret counsel of this heinous treason, with whom he lay nightly, and namely the night last passed next before his death; so that it was the less marvel if ungracious living brought him to an unhappy ending—which he was now put unto, by the most dread commandment of the king's highness and of his honorable and faithful council; both for his demerits, being so openly taken in his falsely conceived treason, and also lest the delaying of his execution might have encouraged other mischievous persons, partners of his conspiracy, to gather and assemble themself together in making some great commotion for his deliverance; whose hope now being by his well deserved death politicly[8] repressed, all the realm should by God's grace rest in good quiet and peace.

Now was this proclamation made within two hours after that he was beheaded, and it was so curiously indited[9] and so fair written in parchment in so well a set[1] hand, and therewith of itself so long a process,[2] that every child might well perceive that

5. *pill and spoil:* rob and kill.   6. pleased.   7. perversion.
8. shrewdly.   9. *curiously indited:* elaborately composed.
1. *well a set:* professional a.   2. narration.

it was prepared before. For all the time between his death and the proclaiming could scant have sufficed unto the bare writing alone, all had it been but in paper and scribbled forth in haste at adventure. So that upon the proclaiming thereof, one that was schoolmaster of Paul's, of chance standing by and comparing the shortness of the time with the length of the matter, said unto them that stood about him, "Here is a gay, goodly cast,[3] foul[4] cast away for haste." And a merchant answered him that it was written by prophecy.

Now then, by and by,[5] as it were for anger, not for covetise,[6] the protector sent into the house of Shore's wife (for her husband dwelled not with her) and spoiled her of all that ever she had, above the value of[7] two or three thousand marks,[8] and sent her body to prison. And when he had awhile laid unto her[9] for the manner sake[1] that she went about to bewitch him and that she was of counsel with the lord chamberlain to destroy him; in conclusion, when that no color[2] could fasten upon these matters, then he laid heinously to her charge the thing that herself could not deny, that all the world wist was true, and that nevertheless every man laughed at to hear it then so suddenly so highly[3] taken—that she was naught[4] of her body.

And for this cause (as a goodly continent[5] prince, clean and faultless of himself, sent out of heaven into this vicious world for the amendment of men's manners) he caused the Bishop of London[6] to put her to open penance, going before the cross in procession upon a Sunday, with a taper in her hand; in which she went in countenance and pace demure so womanly, and albeit she were out of all array[7] save her kirtle[8] only, yet went she so fair and lovely, namely while the wondering of the people

---

3. trick.   4. badly.   5. *by and by:* shortly.   6. covetousness.
7. *above . . . of:* more than.   8. The mark was worth 13s. 4d.
9. *laid . . . her:* brought charges against her.
1. *for . . . sake:* for the sake of appearances.
2. excuse.   3. seriously.   4. immoral.   5. chaste.
6. Thomas Kemp (c. 1414–89).
7. *out . . . array:* without any attire.   8. outer petticoat.

cast a comely rud[9] in her cheeks (of which she before had most miss), that her great shame won her much praise among those that were more amorous of her body than curious of[1] her soul. And many good folk also, that hated her living and glad were to see sin corrected, yet pitied they more her penance than rejoiced therein, when they considered that the protector procured it more of a corrupt intent than any virtuous affection.

This woman was born in London, worshipfully friended,[2] honestly brought up, and very well married (saving somewhat too soon), her husband an honest citizen, young and goodly and of good substance.[3] But forasmuch as they were coupled ere she were well ripe, she not very fervently loved for whom she never longed. Which was haply the thing that the more easily made her incline unto the king's appetite when he required her. Howbeit, the respect of his royalty, the hope of gay apparel, ease, pleasure, and other wanton wealth was soon able to pierce a soft, tender heart. But when the king had abused her, anon her husband (as he was an honest man and one that could his good,[4] not presuming to touch a king's concubine) left her up to him altogether. When the king died, the lord chamberlain took her, which in the king's days, albeit he was sore enamored upon her, yet he forbare her, either for reverence or for a certain friendly faithfulness.

Proper[5] she was and fair, nothing in her body that you would have changed, but if you would have wished her somewhat higher. Thus say they that knew her in her youth, albeit some that now see her (for yet she liveth)[6] deem her never to have been well visaged. Whose judgment seemeth me somewhat like as though men should guess the beauty of one long before departed by her scalp, taken out of the charnel house; for now is

9. red color.   1. *curious of:* concerned for.

2. *worshipfully friended:* with worthy friends.

3. wealth.   4. *could his good:* knew what was good for him.

5. Good-looking.

6. Jane Shore was, according to More's Latin text, in her seventies around 1513; she would thus have been born in the early 1440s.

she old, lean, withered, and dried up, nothing left but rivelled[7] skin and hard bone. And yet, being even such, whoso well advise[8] her visage, might guess and devise which parts, how filled, would make it a fair face.

Yet delighted not men so much in her beauty as in her pleasant behavior. For a proper[9] wit had she, and could both read well and write, merry in company, ready and quick of answer, neither mute nor full of babble, sometime taunting without displeasure and not without disport.[1] The king would say that he had three concubines, which in three divers properties diversely excelled: one the merriest, another the wiliest, the third the holiest harlot in his realm, as one whom no man could get out of church lightly[2] to any place, but it were to his bed. The other two[3] were somewhat greater personages, and nevertheless of their humility content to be nameless and to forbear the praise of those properties. But the merriest was this Shore's wife, in whom the king therefore took special pleasure. For many he had, but her he loved, whose favor, to say truth (for sin it were to belie the devil), she never abused to any man's hurt, but to many a man's comfort and relief; where the king took displeasure, she would mitigate and appease his mind; where men were out of favor, she would bring them in his grace; for many that highly offended, she obtained pardon. Of great forfeitures she gat[4] men remission. And finally, in many weighty suits, she stood many men in good stead; either for none or very small rewards, and those rather gay than rich, either for that she was content with the deed self well done; or for that she delighted to be sued unto and to show what she was able to do with the king; or for that wanton women and wealthy be not alway covetous.

I doubt not some shall think this woman too slight a thing to be written of and set among the remembrances of great matters, which they shall specially think that haply shall esteem

7. wrinkled. 8. observe. 9. excellent. 1. merriment.
2. easily.
3. Edward had many mistresses, but the references here are probably to Eleanor Butler and Elizabeth Lucy. 4. got.

her only by that[5] they now see her. But me seemeth the chance[6] so much the more worthy to be remembered, in how much she is now in the more beggarly condition, unfriended and worn out of acquaintance, after good substance, after as great favor with the prince, after as great suit and seeking to with all those that those days had business to speed, as many other men were in their times, which be now famous only by the infamy of their ill deeds. Her doings were not much less, albeit they be much less remembered because they were not so evil. For men use,[7] if they have an evil turn, to write it in marble, and whoso doth us a good turn, we write it in dust; which is not worst proved by her, for at this day she beggeth of many at this day living, that at this day had begged if she had not been.

Now was it so devised by the protector and his council that the self day[8] in which the lord chamberlain was beheaded in the Tower of London, and about the selfsame hour, was there (not without his assent) beheaded at Pomfret the fore remembered[9] lords and knights that were taken from the king at Northampton and Stony Stratford. Which thing was done in the presence and by the order of Sir Richard Radcliff,[1] knight, whose service the protector specially used in the council and in the execution of such lawless enterprises, as a man that had been long secret with him, having experience of the world and a shrewd wit, short and rude in speech, rough and boustious[2] of behavior, bold in mischief, as far from pity as from all fear of God. This knight, bringing them out of the prison to the scaffold, and showing to the people about that they were traitors, not suffering them to speak and declare their innocence, lest their words might have inclined men to pity them and to hate the protector and his part,[3] caused them hastily, without judgment, process,[4] or

5. the condition in which.   6. story.
7. are accustomed.   8. Actually, not until June 25.
9. *fore remembered:* previously mentioned.
1. Sir Richard Radcliff, a strong and well-rewarded supporter of Richard, died at Bosworth (1485).
2. coarse.   3. side, party.   4. legal action.

manner of order, to be beheaded, and without other earthly guilt but only that they were good men, too true to the king and too nigh[5] to the queen.

Now when the lord chamberlain and these other lords and knights were thus beheaded and rid out of the way, then thought the protector, that while men mused what the matter meant, while the lords of the realm were about him, out of their own strengths,[6] while no man wist what to think nor whom to trust, ere ever they should have space to dispute and disgest[7] the matter and make parties; it were best hastily to pursue his purpose and put himself in possession of the crown, ere men could have time to devise any ways to resist. But now was all the study by what means this matter, being of itself so heinous, might be first broken to the people, in such wise that it might be well taken. To this counsel they took diverse, such as they thought meetly to be[8] trusted, likely to be induced to the part,[9] and able to stand them in stead, either by power or policy.

Among whom they made of counsel[1] Edmund Shaa, knight, then Mayor of London, which upon trust of his own advancement, whereof he was of a proud heart highly desirous, should frame[2] the city to their appetite. Of spiritual men they took such as had wit and were in authority among the people for opinion of their learning and had no scrupulous conscience. Among these had they John Shaa,[3] clerk, brother to the mayor, and Friar Penker,[4] Provincial of the Augustine Friars, both doctors of divinity, both great preachers, both of more learning than virtue, of more fame than learning. For they were before greatly esteemed among the people, but after that never.

Of these two the one had a sermon in praise of the protector before the coronation, the other after; both so full of tedious

5. closely related.
6. *out . . . strengths:* away from their own strongholds.
7. ponder.   8. *meetly to be:* could be suitably.
9. *the part:* their side.   1. *made of counsel:* took into confidence.
2. dispose.
3. i.e., *Ralph* Shaa (d. 1484?).   4. Thomas Penker (d. 1487).

flattery that no man's ears could abide them. Penker in his
sermon so lost his voice that he was fain to leave off and come
down in the midst. Doctor Shaa by his sermon lost his honesty
and soon after his life, for very shame of the world, into which
he durst never after come abroad. But the friar forced[5] for no
shame, and so it harmed him the less. Howbeit, some doubt and
many thinken that Penker was not of counsel of the matter before the coronation, but, after the common manner,[6] fell to
flattery after; namely sith[7] his sermon was not incontinent
upon[8] it, but at Saint Mary Hospital at the Easter after.[9] But
certain is it that Doctor Shaa was of counsel in the beginning so
far forth that they determined that he should first break the
matter in a sermon at Paul's Cross, in which he should by the
authority of his preaching incline the people to the protector's
ghostly[1] purpose.

But now was all the labor and study in the devise[2] of some
convenient pretext for which the people should be content to
depose the prince and accept the protector for king. In which
divers things they devised. But the chief thing and the weighty of
all that invention rested in this: that they should allege bastardy,
either in King Edward himself, or in his children, or both, so
that he should seem disabled to inherit the crown by the Duke
of York, and the prince by him. To lay bastardy in King Edward
sounded[3] openly to the rebuke of the protector's own mother,[4]
which was mother to them both; for in that point could be none
other color[5] but to pretend that his own mother was one adulter-
ess, which not withstanding to further this purpose he letted[6]

5. cared.
6. *after ... manner:* in imitation of the common behavior.
7. *namely sith:* especially since.
8. *incontinent upon:* immediately after.
9. The Easter sermons (begun on Good Friday and continued during
Easter Week) were preached in a courtyard attached to the hospital.
1. shadowy.   2. devising.   3. tended.
4. Cecily, Duchess of York (d. 1495), the sister of Warwick's father,
Richard Neville.   5. pretext.   6. refrained.

not. But nevertheless, he would the point should be less and more favorably handled, not even fully plain and directly; but that the matter should be touched a slope,[7] craftily, as though men spared in that point to speak all the truth for fear of his displeasure. But the other point, concerning the bastardy that they devised to surmise in King Edward's children—that, would he, should be openly declared and enforced to the uttermost.

The color and pretext whereof cannot be well perceived but if we first repeat you some things long before done about King Edward's marriage.[8] After that King Edward the Fourth had deposed King Henry the Sixth and was in peaceable possession of the realm, determining himself to marry (as it was requisite both for himself and for the realm), he sent over in embassiate[9] the Earl of Warwick[1] with other noble men in his company unto Spain, to entreat and conclude a marriage between King Edward and the king's daughter of Spain.[2] In which thing the Earl of Warwick found the parties so toward[3] and willing that he speedily, according to his instructions, without any difficulty brought the matter to a very good conclusion.

Now happed it that in the mean season[4] there came, to make a suit by petition to the king, Dame Elizabeth Grey—which was after his queen, at that time a widow—born of noble blood, specially by her mother, which was Duchess of Bedford ere she married the Lord Woodville,[5] her father. Howbeit, this Dame Elizabeth, herself being in service with Queen Margaret,[6] wife

---

7. *a slope:* obliquely.
8. Edward IV married Elizabeth Woodville in 1464.   9. embassy.
1. Richard Neville, Earl of Warwick and Salisbury (1428–71), first cousin of Edward IV; a man of great power, he was known as the "king-maker."
2. Isabella (1451–1504) sister of Henry the Impotent, King of Castile, and adopted heiress to his throne.
3. obliging.   4. meantime.
5. Elizabeth's mother, Jacquetta, married Henry V's brother John in 1433 and, after his death, Sir Richard Woodville.
6. Margaret of Anjou (1429–82).

unto King Henry the Sixth, was married unto one John Grey,[7] a squire, whom King Henry made knight upon the field that he had on Shrove Tuesday at Saint Albans against King Edward. And little while enjoyed he that knighthood, for he was at the same field slain. After which done, and the Earl of Warwick being in his embassiate about the afore remembered marriage, this poor lady made humble suit unto the king that she might be restored unto such small lands as her late husband had given her in jointure.[8]

Whom, when the king beheld and heard her speak—as she was both fair, of a good favor,[9] moderate of stature, well made, and very wise—he not only pitied her, but also waxed enamored on her. And taking her afterward secretly aside, began to enter in talking more familiarly. Whose appetite when she perceived, she virtuously denied him. But that did she so wisely, and with so good manner, and words so well set, that she rather kindled his desire than quenched it. And finally, after many a meeting, much wooing, and many great promises, she well espied the king's affection toward her so greatly increased that she durst somewhat the more boldly say her mind, as to him whose heart she perceived more firmly set than to fall off for a word. And in conclusion she showed him plain that as she wist herself too simple to be his wife, so thought she herself too good to be his concubine. The king, much marvelling of her constaunce,[1] as he that had not been wont elsewhere to be so stiffly said nay, so much esteemed her continence and chastity that he set her virtue in the stead of possession and riches. And thus taking counsel of his desire, determined in all possible haste to marry her.

And after he was thus appointed[2] and had between them twain ensured[3] her, then asked he counsel of his other friends,

7. Sir John Grey (1432–61), who had married Elizabeth about 1452; Henry VI was not at the battle of St. Albans (1461) and Grey had already been knighted in 1458.
8. The holding of property to the joint use of a husband and wife.
9. appearance.
1. constancy.   2. resolved.   3. betrothed.

and that in such manner as they might ethe[4] perceive it booted
not greatly to say nay. Notwithstanding, the Duchess of York,
his mother, was so sore moved therewith that she dissuaded the
marriage as much as she possibly might, alleging that it was his
honor, profit, and surety also, to marry in a noble progeny[5] out
of his realm, whereupon depended great strength to his estate
by the affinity[6] and great possibility of increase of his possessions; and that he could not well otherwise do, standing[7] that
the Earl of Warwick had so far moved already—which were not
likely to take it well, if all his voyage were in such wise frustrate
and his appointments deluded.[8]

And she said also that it was not princely to marry his own
subject, no great occasion leading thereunto, no possessions or
other commodities depending thereupon, but only, as it were,
a rich man that would marry his maid only for a little wanton
dotage upon her person. In which marriage, many more commend the maiden's fortune than the master's wisdom. And yet
therein she said was more honesty than honor in this marriage,
forasmuch as there is between no merchant and his own maid
so great difference as between the king and this widow. In
whose person, albeit there was nothing to be misliked, yet was
there, she said, "nothing so excellent but that it might be
founden in diverse other that were more meetly,"[9] quod she,
"for your estate,[1] and maidens also; whereas the only widowhood[2] of Elizabeth Grey, though she were in all other things
convenient[3] for you, should yet suffice, as me seemeth, to refrain you from marriage, sith it is an unsitting[4] thing, and a
very blemish and high disparagement to the sacred majesty of
a prince, that ought as nigh to approach priesthood in cleanness
as he doth in dignity, to be defouled with bigamy[5] in his first
marriage."

4. easily.   5. family.   6. relationship.   7. considering.
8. *appointments deluded:* agreements thwarted.
9. suitable.   1. rank in society.
2. *only widowhood:* widowhood alone.   3. suitable.
4. unbecoming.   5. marriage to a widow.

The king, when his mother had said,[6] made her answer, part
in earnest, part in play merrily, as he that wist himself out of her
rule. And albeit he would gladly that she should take it well, yet
was at a point[7] in his own mind, took she it well or otherwise.
Howbeit, somewhat to satisfy her, he said that albeit marriage,
being a spiritual thing, ought rather to be made for the respect
of God, where his grace inclineth the parties to love together, as
he trusted it was in his, than for the regard of any temporal
advantage; yet nevertheless, him seemed that this marriage,
even worldly considered, was not unprofitable. For he reckoned
the amity of no earthly nation so necessary for him as the friendship of his own, which he thought likely to bear him so much
the more hearty favor in that he disdained not to marry with
one of his own land. And yet, if outward[8] alliance were thought
so requisite, he would find the means to enter thereinto much
better by other of his kin, where all the parties could be contented, than to marry himself whom he should haply never love,
and for the possibility of more possessions, lose the fruit and
pleasure of this that he had already. "For small pleasure taketh
a man of all that ever he hath beside, if he be wived against
his appetite."

"And I doubt not," quod he, "but there be, as ye say, other
that be in every point comparable with her. And therefore I
let[9] not them that like them to wed them. No more is it reason
that it mislike any man that I marry where it liketh me. And
I am sure that my cousin of Warwick neither loveth me so little
to grudge at that I love, nor is so unreasonable to look[1] that I
should in choice of a wife, rather be ruled by his eye than by
mine own, as though I were a ward that were bound to marry by
the appointment of a guardian. I would not be a king with that
condition, to forbear mine own liberty in choice of my own
marriage. As for possibility of more inheritance by new affinity
in strange lands, [it] is oft the occasion of more trouble than

6. spoken.   7. *at a point:* determined.   8. foreign.
9. hinder.   1. expect.

profit. And we have already title by that means to so much as sufficeth to get and keep well in one man's days. That she is a widow and hath already children, by God's blessed lady, I am a bachelor and have some too;[2] and so each of us hath a proof that neither of us is like to be barren. And therefore, madam, I pray you be content. I trust in God she shall bring forth a young prince that shall please you. And as for the bigamy, let the bishop hardly[3] lay it in my way when I come to take orders. For I undersand it is forbidden a priest, but I never wist it yet that it was forbidden a prince."

The duchess, with these words nothing appeased, and seeing the king so set thereon that she could not pull him back, so highly she disdained it that, under pretext of her duty to Godward, she devised to disturb this marriage, and rather to help that he should marry one Dame Elizabeth Lucy, whom the king had also not long before gotten with child. Wherefore the king's mother objected openly against his marriage, as it were in discharge of her conscience, that the king was sure[4] to Dame Elizabeth Lucy and her husband before God. By reason of which words, such obstacle was made in the matter that either the bishops durst not, or the king would not, proceed to the solemnization of his wedding till these same were clearly purged and the truth well and openly testified. Whereupon Dame Elizabeth Lucy was sent for. And albeit that she was by the king's mother and many other put in good comfort to affirm that she was ensured unto the king, yet when she was solemnly sworn to say the truth, she confessed that they were never ensured. Howbeit, she said his grace spoke so loving words unto her that she verily hoped he would have married her, and if it had not been for such kind words she would never have showed such kindness to him to let him so kindly[5] get her with child. This examination solemnly taken, when it was clearly perceived

2. Edward IV's illegitimate children included a son, Arthur Planta-genet (1480–1542), by Elizabeth Lucy and a daughter Elizabeth, born about the time of his marriage.
3. by all means.   4. betrothed.   5. i.e., "naturally."

that there was none impediment, the king, with great feast and honorable solemnity,[6] married Dame Elizabeth Grey and her crowned queen that was his enemy's wife and many time had prayed full heartily for his loss. In which God loved her better than to grant her her boon.

But when the Earl of Warwick understood of this marriage, he took it so highly[7] that his embassiate was deluded[8] that for very anger and disdain he, at his return, assembled a great puissaunce[9] against the king and came so fast upon him, or[1] he could be able to resist, that he was fain to void[2] the realm and flee into Holland for succor, where he remained for the space of two years,[3] leaving his new wife in Westminster in sanctuary, where she was delivered of Edward, the prince, of whom we before have spoken. In which mean time the Earl of Warwick took out of prison and set up again King Henry the Sixth, which was before by King Edward deposed and that much what by the power of the Earl of Warwick,[4] which was a wise man and a courageous warrior and of such strength, what for his lands, his alliance,[5] and favor with all the people, that he[6] made kings and put down kings almost at his pleasure, and not impossible to have attained it himself, if he had not reckoned it a greater thing to make a king than to be a king. But nothing lasteth alway; for in conclusion King Edward returned, and with much less number than he had, at Barnet on the Easter Day field,[7] slew the Earl of Warwick with many other great estates of that party, and so stably[8] attained the crown again that he peaceably enjoyed it until his dying day, and in such

6. More seems to describe Elizabeth's coronation in 1465, not her secret marriage in 1464.

7. indignantly.   8. frustrated.   9. armed force.

1. before.   2. depart from.

3. Warwick drove Edward out in 1470; he was absent from the realm for only five months and eleven days.

4. *much . . . Warwick:* i.e., Warwick had also had a strong hand in the original deposition of Henry VI.

5. family relationships.   6. i.e., Warwick.

7. April 14, 1471.   8. solidly.

plight[9] left it that it could not be lost but by the discord of his
very friends or falsehood of his feigned friends.

I have rehearsed this business about this marriage somewhat
the more at length because it might thereby the better appear
upon how slipper[1] a ground the protector builded his color by
which he pretended King Edward's childen to be bastards.
But that invention, simple as it was—it liked them to whom it
sufficed to have somewhat to say, while they were sure to be
compelled to no larger proof than themself list[2] to make. Now
then, as I began to show you, it was by the protector and his
council concluded that this Doctor Shaa should in a sermon at
Paul's Cross signify to the people that neither King Edward
himself nor the Duke of Clarence were lawfully begotten, nor
were not the very children of the Duke of York, but gotten
unlawfully by other persons by the adultery of the duchess,
their mother; and that also Dame Elizabeth Lucy was verily
the wife of King Edward, and so the prince and all his children
bastards that were gotten upon the queen.

According to this device,[3] Doctor Shaa, the Sunday after,[4]
at Paul's Cross in a great audience (as alway assembled great
number to his preaching), he took for his tyme[5] *Spuria vitula-
mina non agent radices altas,*[6] that is to say "bastard slips shall
never take deep root." Thereupon, when he had showed the
great grace that God giveth and secretly infoundeth[7] in right
generation after the laws of matrimony, then declared he that
commonly those children lacked that grace, and for the punishment of their parents, were for the more part unhappy, which
were gotten in baste[8] and specially in adultery. Of which,
though some by the ignorance of the world and the truth hid
fro knowledge inherited for the season other men's lands, yet
God alway so provideth that it continueth not in their blood

9. good condition.   1. unstable.   2. pleased.   3. scheme.
4. *Sunday after:* i.e., after Hastings' death. But the sermon was actually given on June 22, not June 15.
5. theme, text of a sermon.   6. *Spuria . . . altas: Wisdom* 4:3.
7. infuses.   8. bastardy.

long, but the truth coming to light, the rightful inheritors be restored and the bastard slip pulled up ere it can be rooted deep.

And when he had laid for the proof and confirmation of this sentence certain examples taken out of the Old Testament and other ancient histories, then began he to descend into the praise of the Lord Richard, late Duke of York, calling him father to the lord protector, and declared the title of his heirs unto the crown, to whom it was, after the death of King Henry the Sixth, entailed by authority of parliament. Then showed he that his very right heir of his body, lawfully begotten, was only the lord protector, for he declared then that King Edward was never lawfully married unto the queen, but was, before God, husband unto Dame Elizabeth Lucy, and so his children bastards. And besides that, neither King Edward himself, nor the Duke of Clarence, among those that were secret[9] in the household, were reckoned very surely for the children of the noble duke, as those that by their favors[1] more resembled other known men than him, from whose virtuous conditions[2] he said also that King Edward was far off. But the lord protector, he said, that very noble prince, the special pattern of knightly prowess, as well in all princely behavior as in the lineaments[3] and favor of his visage, represented the very face of the noble duke, his father. "This is," quod he, "the father's own figure; this is his own countenance—the very print of his visage, the sure undoubted image, the plain express likeness of that noble duke."

Now was it before devised that in the speaking of these words the protector should have comen in among the people to the sermonward,[4] to the end that those words, meeting with his presence, might have been taken among the hearers as though the Holy Ghost had put them in the preacher's mouth and should have moved the people even there to cry, "King Richard! King Richard!"—that it might have been after said

9. intimate.   1. physical appearances.   2. morals.
3. features.   4. *to the sermonward:* to hear the sermon.

that he was specially chosen by God and in manner[5] by miracle. But this devise quailed,[6] either by the protector's negligence or the preacher's overmuch diligence. For while the protector found by the way tarrying,[7] lest he should prevent[8] those words, and the doctor, fearing that he should come ere his sermon could come to those words, hasted his matter thereto; he was come to them and past them and entered into other matters ere the protector came. Whom when he beheld coming, he suddenly left the matter with which he was in hand, and without any deduction[9] thereunto, out of all order and out of all frame, began to repeat those words again: "This is the very noble prince, the special patron of knightly prowess, which as well in all princely behavior, as in the lineaments and favor of his visage representeth the very face of the noble Duke of York, his father. This is the father's own figure, this his own countenance, the very print of his visage, the sure undoubted image, the plain express likeness of the noble duke, whose remembrance can never die while he liveth."

While these words were in speaking, the protector, accompanied wtih the Duke of Buckingham, went through the people into the place where the doctors commonly stand in the upper story, where he stood to harken the sermon. But the people were so far fro crying "King Richard!" that they stood as they had been turned into stone, for wonder of this shameful sermon. After which once ended, the preacher gat him home and never after durst look out for shame, but kept him out of sight like an owl. And when he once asked one that had been his old friend what the people talked of him, all were it that[1] his own conscience well showed him that they talked no good, yet when the other answered him that there was in every man's mouth spoken of him much shame, it so strake[2] him to the heart that within few days after, he withered and consumed away.

5. *in manner:* as it were.
6. failed.   7. *found . . . tarrying:* contrived delays on the way.
8. arrive before.   9. introduction.
1. *all . . . that:* even though.   2. struck.

Then, on the Tuesday[3] following this sermon, there came unto the Guildhall in London the Duke of Buckingham, accompanied with divers lords and knights, more than haply knew the message that they brought. And there, in the east end of the hall where the mayor keepeth the hustings,[4] the mayor and all the aldermen being assembled about him, all the commons of the city gathered before them, after silence commanded upon great pain in the protector's name, the duke stood up, and (as he was neither unlearned and of nature marvelously well spoken) he said unto the people with a clear and a loud voice in this manner of wise:

"Friends, for the zeal and hearty favor that we bear you, we be comen to break unto you of a matter right great and weighty, and no less weighty than pleasing to God and profitable to all the realm, nor to no part of the realm more profitable than to you, the citizens of this noble city. For why?[5] That thing that we wot[6] well ye have long time lacked and sore[7] longed for, that ye would have given great good for, that ye would have gone far to fetch—that thing we be come hither to bring you, without your labor, pain, cost, adventure, or jeopardy. What thing is that? Certes,[8] the surety of your own bodies, the quiet of your wives and your daughters, the safeguard of your goods—of all which things, in times passed, ye stood evermore in doubt. For who was there of you all that would reckon himself lord of his own good, among so many grennes[9] and traps as was set therefor, among so much pilling and polling,[1] among so many taxes and tallages,[2] of which there was never end and oftentime no need, or if any were, it rather grew of riot and unreasonable waste than any necessary or honorable charge. So that there was daily pilled fro good

4. i.e., the Court of Hustings, the highest tribunal for London.
5. *For why?:* For what reason?   6. know.   7. exceedingly.
8. Certainly.   9. snares.
1. *pilling and polling:* plundering and robbing.
2. arbitrary impositions.

men and honest, great substance of goods to be lashed out[3] among unthrifts so farforth that fifteenths[4] sufficed not, nor any usual names of known taxes, but under an easy name of benevolence and good will, the commissioners so much of every man took as no man would with his good will have given—as though the name of benevolence had signified that every man should pay, not what himself of his good will list to grant, but what the king of his good will list to take; which never asked little, but everything was hawsed[5] above the measure: amercements[6] turned into fines, fines into ransom, small trespass to misprision,[7] misprision into treason.

"Whereof, I think, no man looketh that we should remember[8] you of examples by name, as though Burdet[9] were forgotten, that was for a word spoken in haste, cruelly beheaded by the misconstruing of the law of this realm for the prince's pleasure; with no less honor to Markham,[1] then chief justice, that left his office rather than he would assent to that judgment, than to the dishonesty of those that either for fear or flattery gave that judgment. What[2] Cook,[3] your own worshipful neighbor, alderman and mayor of this noble city? Who is of you either so negligent that he knoweth not, or so forgetful that he remembereth not, or so hardhearted that he pitieth not that

3. *lashed out:* squandered.
4. A tax of one-fifteenth imposed on personal property.   5. raised.
6. An arbitrary fine (originally lighter in amount than fines fixed for specific offenses).
7. Offense akin to treason but not involving capital punishment.
8. remind.
9. Thomas Burdet (1420–77) was executed (according to one tale) for uttering a rash word against the king when Edward killed a pet buck.
1. Sir John Markham (d. 1479), chief justice from 1461, actually resigned office over the Cook case (see below).
2. What of.
3. Sir Thomas Cook (1420–78) a prosperous London draper, mayor in 1462, was impeached of high treason in 1467 for lending money to Queen Margaret.

worshipful man's loss? What speak we of loss? his utter spoil[4]
and undeserved destruction, only for that it happed those to
favor him whom the prince favored not. We need not, I suppose, to rehearse of these any more by name, sith there be, I
doubt not, many here present that either in themself or their
nigh friends have known as well their goods as their persons
greatly endangered, either by feigned quarrels or small matters
aggrieved[5] with heinous names.

"And also there was no crime so great of which there could
lack a pretext. For sith the king, preventing[6] the time of his
inheritance, attained the crown by battle, it sufficed in a rich
man for a pretext of treason to have been of kindred or alliance,
near familiarity or leger[7] acquaintance with any of those that
were at any time the king's enemies, which was at one time and
other, more than half the realm. Thus were neither your goods
in surety and yet they brought your bodies in jeopardy—beside
the common adventure of open war, which albeit that it is ever
the will and occasion of much mischief, yet is it never so mischievous as where any people fall at distance[8] among themself,
nor in none earthly nation so deadly and so pestilent as when it
happeneth among us, and among us never so long continued
dissension, nor so many battles in the season, nor so cruel and
so deadly foughten, as was in the king's days that dead is, God
forgive it his soul. In whose time and by whose occasion,[9] what
about the getting of the garland, keeping it, losing and winning
again, it hath cost more English blood than hath twice the winning of France. In which inward war among ourself hath been
so great effusion of the ancient noble blood of this realm that
scarcely the half remaineth, to the great enfeebling of this noble
land, beside many a good town ransacked and spoiled by them
that have been going to the field or coming from thence. And

4. While Cook was in jail, his lands were seized and his houses
plundered.
5. exaggerated.   6. acting before.   7. slight.
8. *at distance:* to discord.   9. action.

peace long after not much surer than war. So that no time was there in which rich men for their money and great men for their lands, or some other for some fear or some displeasure were not out of peril. For whom trusted he that mistrusted his own brother? Whom spared he that killed his own brother?[1] Or who could perfectly love him, if his own brother could not?

"What manner of folk he most favored, we shall, for his honor, spare to speak of; howbeit, this wot you well all, that who so was best, bare alway least rule, and more suit was in his days unto Shore's wife, a vile and an abominable strumpet, than to all the lords in England—except unto those that made her their proctor[2]—which simple woman was well named and honest till the king, for his wanton lust and sinful affection, bereft her from her husband, a right honest, substantial[3] young man among you. And in that point, which in good faith I am sorry to speak of, saving that it is in vain to keep in counsel that thing that all men know: the king's greedy appetite was insatiable and everywhere over all the realm intolerable. For no woman was there anywhere, young or old, rich or poor, whom he set his eye upon, in whom he anything liked, either person or favor,[4] speech, pace, or countenance, but without any fear of God or respect of his honor, murmur or grudge of the world, he would importunely[5] pursue his appetite and have her, to the great destruction of many a good woman and great dolor[6] to their husband and their other friends, which being honest people of themself so much regard the cleanness of their house, the chastity of their wives and their children that them were lever[7] to lose all that they have beside than to have such a villainy done them.

"And all were it that with this and other importable[8] dealing the realm was in every part annoyed, yet specially ye here, the citizens of this noble city, as well for that among you is most

1. *killed . . . brother:* A reference to Edward's execution of Clarence.
2. advocate.   3. wealthy.   4. appearance.
5. solicitously.   6. sorrow.
7. *them were lever:* they would prefer.   8. unbearable.

plenty of all such things as minister[9] matter to such injuries, as
for that you were nearest at hand, sith that near here about was
commonly his most abiding. And yet be ye the people whom he
had as singular cause well and kindly to entreat[1] as any part of
his realm, not only for that the prince by this noble city (as his
special chamber and the special well-renowned city of his
realm), much honorable fame receiveth among all other nations; but also for that ye, not without your great cost and
sundry perils and jeopardies in all his wars, bare ever your
special favor to his part, which with your kind minds borne[2] to
the House of York (sith he hath nothing worthily acquitted),[3]
there is of that house that[4] now, by God's grace, better shall—
which thing to show you is the whole sum and effect of this our
present errand.

"It shall not, I wot well, need that I rehearse you again that
ye have already heard of[5] him that can better tell it, and of
whom, I am sure, ye will better believe it. And reason is that it
so be. I am not so proud to look therefore that ye should
reckon my words of as great authority as the preachers of the
word of God, namely, a man so cunning[6] and so wise that no
man better woteth what he should say, and thereto so good and
virtuous that he would not say the thing which he wist he should
not say, in the pulpit namely, into which none honest man
cometh to lie. Which honorable preacher ye well remember
substantially[7] declared unto you at Paul's Cross on Sunday last
passed the right and title that the most excellent Prince,
Richard, Duke of Gloucester, now protector of this realm, hath
unto the crown and kingdom of the same.

"For as that worshipful man groundly[8] made open unto you,
the children of King Edward the Fourth were never lawfully
begotten, forasmuch as the king (living his very[9] wife, Dame

9. furnish. 1. treat. 2. entertained. 3. accomplished.
4. *of that house that:* i.e., a man of that house who.
5. from. 6. learned. 7. thoroughly. 8. thoroughly.
9. true.

Elizabeth Lucy) was never lawfully married unto the queen, their mother, whose blood, saving that he set his voluptuous pleasure before his honor, was full unmeetly[1] to be matched with his; and the mingling of whose blood together hath been the effusion of great part of the noble blood of this realm. Whereby it may well seem that marriage not well made, of which there is so much mischief grown. For lack of which lawful accoupling[2] and also of other things which the said worshipful doctor rather signified than fully explained, and which things shall not be spoken for me[3] as the thing wherein every man forebeareth to say that he knoweth in avoiding displeasure of my noble lord protector, bearing as nature requireth a filial reverence to the duchess, his mother—for these causes, I say, before remembered, that is to wit, for lack of other issue lawfully coming of the late noble prince, Richard, Duke of York, to whose royal blood the crown of England and of France is by the high authority of parliament entailed—the right and title of the same is by the just course of inheritance, according to the common law of this land, devolute[4] and comen unto the most excellent prince, the lord protector, as to the very lawfully begotten son of the fore-remembered noble Duke of York.

"Which thing well considered, and the great knightly prowess pondered, with manifold virtues which in his noble person singularly abound, the nobles and commons also of this realm, and specially of the north parts, not willing any bastard blood to have the rule of the land, nor the abusions[5] before in the same used any longer to continue, have condescended[6] and fully determined to make humble petition unto the most puissant prince, the lord protector, that it may like his grace, at our humble request, to take upon him the guiding and governance of this realm to the wealth and increase of the same, according to his very right and just title. Which thing, I wot it well, he

---

1. unsuitable.   2. union in marriage.
3. *for me:* on my part.   4. transmitted down.
5. outrages.   6. agreed together.

will be loath to take upon him, as he whose wisdom well perceiveth the labor and study both of mind and of body that shall come therewith to whomsoever so well occupy that room,[7] as I dare say he will if he take it. Which room, I warn you well, is no child's office. And that the great wise man[8] well perceived when he said, *Veh regno cuius rex puer est.* 'Woe is that realm that hath a child to[9] their king.'

"Wherefore, so much the more cause have we to thank God that this noble personage, which is so righteously entitled thereunto, is of so sad[1] age and thereto of so great wisdom joined with so great experience; which albeit he will be loath, as I have said, to take it upon him, yet shall he to our petition in that behalf the more graciously incline, if ye, the worshipful citizens of this the chief city of this realm, join with us, the nobles, in our said request. Which for your own weal[2] we doubt not but ye will, and nevertheless, I heartily pray you so to do, whereby you shall do great profit to all this realm beside in choosing them so good a king, and unto yourself special commodity,[3] to whom his majesty shall ever after bear so much the more tender favor, in how much he shall perceive you the more prone and benevolently minded toward his election. Wherein, dear friends, what mind you have, we require you plainly to show us."

When the duke had said, and looked that the people, whom he hoped that the mayor had framed[4] before, should after this proposition made have cried "King Richard! King Richard!"—all was hushed and mute and not one word answered thereunto. Wherewith the duke was marvelously abashed, and taking the mayor nearer to him, with other that were about him privy to that matter, said unto them softly, "What meaneth this that this people be so still?"

7. office.
8. Solomon, the reputed author of *Ecclesiastes;* Buckingham quotes *Eccles.* 10 : 16.
9. as.   1. mature.   2. well-being.   3. advantage.
4. disposed.

"Sir," quod the mayor, "percase[5] they perceive you not well."

"That shall we mend," quod he, "if that will help."

And by and by,[6] somewhat louder, he rehearsed them the same matter again in other order and other words, so well and ornately, and nevertheless, so evidently and plain, with voice, gesture, and countenance so comely and so convenient[7] that every man much marvelled that heard him and thought that they never had in their lives heard so evil a tale so well told. _sophist_ But were it for wonder or fear, or that each look[8] that other should speak first, not one word was there answered of all the people that stood before, but all was as still as the midnight, not so much as rowning[9] among them by which they might seem to comen[1] what was best to do.

When the mayor saw this, he with other partners of that counsel drew about the duke and said that the people had not been accustomed there to be spoken unto but by the recorder,[2] which is the mouth of the city, and haply to him they will answer. With that the recorder, called Fitzwilliam,[3] a sad[4] man and an honest, which was so new come into that office that he never had spoken to the people before, and loath was with that matter to begin, notwithstanding, thereunto commanded by the mayor, made rehearsal[5] to the commons of that the duke had twice rehearsed them himself. But the recorder so tempered his tale that he showed everything as the duke's words and no part his own. But all this nothing no change[6] made in the people which always after one[7] stood as they had been men amazed.

Whereupon the duke rowned[8] unto the mayor and said, "This is a marvelous obstinate silence."

And therewith he turned unto the people again with these

---

5. perhaps.   6. *by and by:* immediately.   7. fitting.
8. expected.   9. whispering.   1. confer.
2. The mayor's assistant, a well-trained lawyer who guards against errors of judgment made through ignorance of the law.
3. Sir Thomas Fitzwilliam (1427–97).   4. grave.
5. recitation.   6. *nothing no change:* no change at all.
7. *after one:* in harmony with each other.   8. whispered.

words: "Dear friends, we come to move you to that thing which peradventure we not so greatly needed but that the lords of this realm and the commons of other parts might have sufficed, saving that we such love bear you and so much set by[9] you that we would not gladly do without you that thing in which to be partners is your weal[1] and honor, which, as it seemeth, either you see not or weigh not. Wherefore we require you give us answer one or other: whether you be minded, as all the nobles of the realm be, to have this noble prince, now protector, to be your king or not."

At these words the people began to whisper among themself secretly, that the voice was neither loud nor distinct, but as[2] it were the sound of a swarm of bees; till, at the last, in the nether[3] end of the hall a bushment[4] of the duke's servants, and Nesfield's,[5] and other longing[6] to the protector, with some prentices and lads that thrust into the hall among the press,[7] began suddenly at men's backs to cry out as loud as their throats would give, "King Richard! King Richard!"—and threw up their caps in token of joy. And they that stood before cast back their heads, marvelling thereof, but nothing they said. And when the duke and the mayor saw this manner, they wisely turned it to their purpose and said it was a goodly cry and a joyful to hear, every man with one voice, no man saying nay.

"Wherefore, friends," quod the duke, "since that we perceive it is all your whole minds to have this noble man for your king, whereof we shall make his grace so effectual[8] report that we doubt not but it shall redound unto your great weal and commodity, we require ye that ye tomorrow go with us and we with you unto his noble grace to make our humble request unto him in manner before remembered." [9]

And therewith the lords came down, and the company dis-

---

9. *set by:* esteem.   1. well-being.   2. as if.   3. lower.
4. secretly concealed group.
5. John Nesfield of London, who performed and was rewarded for numerous services ordered by Richard.
6. belonging.   7. crowd.   8. effective.   9. mentioned.

solved and departed, the more part all sad, some with glad
semblance that were not very merry; and some of those that
came thither with the duke, not able to dissemble their sorrow,
were fain at his back to turn their face to the wall while the
dolor of their heart braste[1] out at their eyes.

Then on the morrow after,[2] the mayor with all the aldermen
and chief commoners of the city, in their best manner apparelled,
assembling themself together, resorted unto Baynard's Castle,[3]
where the protector lay. To which place repaired also, according to their appointment, the Duke of Buckingham, with divers
noble men with him, beside many knights and other gentlemen.
And thereupon the duke sent word unto the lord protector of
the being there of a great and honorable company to move a
great matter unto his grace. Whereupon the protector made
difficulty to come out unto them, but if[4] he first knew some part
of their errand, as though he doubted and partly distrusted the
coming of such number unto him so suddenly, without any
warning or knowledge whether they came for good or harm.

Then the duke, when he had showed this unto the mayor
and other that they might thereby see how little the protector
looked for this matter, they sent unto him by the messenger such
loving message again and therewith so humbly besought him to
vouchsafe that they might resort to his presence to purpose[5]
their intent, of which they would unto none other person any
part disclose, that at the last he came forth of[6] his chamber;
and yet not down unto them, but stood above in a gallery over
them where they might see him and speak to him, as though
he would not yet come too near them till he wist what they
meant.

And thereupon the Duke of Buckingham first made humble
petition unto him, on the behalf of them all, that his grace
would pardon them and license them to purpose unto his grace
the intent of their coming without his displeasure, without

1. burst.   2. *morrow after:* Wednesday, June 25.
3. *Baynard's Castle:* Residence of Cecily, Duchess of York.
4. *but if:* unless.   5. propose.   6. from.

which pardon obtained, they durst not be bold to move[7] him of that matter. In which, albeit they meant as much honor to his grace as wealth to all the realm beside, yet were they not sure how his grace would take it, whom they would in no wise offend.

Then the protector, as he was very gentle of himself and also longed sore to wit[8] what they meant, gave him leave to purpose what him liked, verily trusting, for the good mind that he bare them all, none of them anything would intend unto him ward[9] wherewith he ought to be grieved. When the duke had this leave and pardon to speak, then waxed he bold to show him their intent and purpose, with all the causes moving them thereunto, as ye before have heard, and finally to beseech his grace that it would like[1] him of his accustomed goodness and zeal unto the realm, now with his eye of pity, to behold the long continued distress and decay of the same and to set his gracious hands to the redress and amendment thereof by taking upon him the crown and governance of this realm, according to his right and title lawfully descended unto him, and to the laud of God, profit of the land, and unto his grace so much the more honor and less pain, in that never prince reigned upon any people that were so glad to live under his obeisance[2] as the people of this realm under his.

When the protector had heard the proposition, he looked very strangely thereat and answered that all were it[3] that he partly knew the things by them alleged to be true, yet such entire love he bare unto King Edward and his children, that so much more regarded his honor in other realms about than the crown of any one, of which he was never desirous, that he could not find in his heart in this point to incline to their desire. For in all other nations where the truth were not well known, it should peradventure be thought that it were his own ambitious mind and devise[4] to depose the prince and take

7. appeal to. 8. know. 9. *unto him ward:* toward him.
1. please. 2. rule. 3. *all . . . it:* although. 4. scheme.

himself the crown. With which infamy he would not have his honor stained for any crown, in which he had ever perceived much more labor and pain than pleasure to him that so would so use it, as he that would not were not worthy to have it.[5] Notwithstanding, he not only pardoned them the motion that they made him, but also thanked them for the love and hearty favor they bare him, praying them for his sake to give and bear the same to the prince, under whom he was and would be content to live; and with his labor and counsel, as far as should like the king to use him, he would do his uttermost devoir[6] to set the realm in good state, which was already in this little while of his protectorship (the praise given to God) well begun, in that the malice of such as were before of the contrary and of new intended to be, were now, partly by good policy, partly more by God's special providence than man's provision, repressed.

Upon this answer given, the duke, by the protector's license, a little rowned,[7] as well with other noble men about him, as with the mayor and recorder of London. And after that, upon like pardon desired and obtained, he showed aloud unto the protector that for a final conclusion that the realm was appointed[8] King Edward's line should not any longer reign upon them, both for that they had so far gone that it was now no surety to retreat, as for that they thought it for the weal universal to take that way, although they had not yet begun it. Wherefore, if it would like his grace to take the crown upon him, they would humbly beseech him thereunto. If he would give them a resolute answer to the contrary, which they would be loath to hear, then must they needs seek and should not fail to find some other noble man that would.

These words much moved the protector, which else, as every man may wit, would never of likelihood have inclined thereunto. But when he saw there was none other way, but that

5. *as he ... have it:* i.e., as he who would not use it in such a way [justly] was not worthy to have it [the crown].
6. *do ... devoir:* make the greatest possible effort.
7. whispered.   8. determined.

either he must take it or else he and his both go fro it, he said
unto the lords and commons:

"Sith we perceive well that all the realm is so set, whereof
we be very sorry that they will not suffer in any wise King
Edward's line to govern them, whom no man earthly can
govern again[9] their wills; and we well also perceive that no
man is there to whom the crown can by so just title appertain
as to ourself, as very right heir, lawfully begotten of the body
of our most dear father, Richard, late Duke of York, to which
title is now joined your election, the nobles and commons of
this realm, which we of all titles possible take for most effectual:[1] we be content and agree favorably to incline to your
petition and request, and according to the same here we take
upon us the royal estate, pre-eminence, and kingdom of the
two noble realms, England and France; the one fro this day
forward by us and our heirs to rule, govern, and defend; the
other, by God's grace and your good help, to get again and
subdue, and establish for ever in due obedience unto this realm
of England, the advancement whereof we never ask of God
longer to live than we intend to procure."

With this there was a great shout crying, "King Richard!
King Richard!" And then the lords went up to the king (for so
was he from that time called), and the people departed, talking diversely of the matter, every man as his fantasy[2] gave him.

But much they talked and marvelled of the manner of this
dealing; that the matter was on both parts made so strange,[3]
as though neither had ever communed with other thereof before, when that themself well wist there was no man so
dull that heard them but he perceived well enough that all the
matter was made[4] between them. Howbeit, some excused that
again and said all must be done in good order though. And
men must sometime for the manner sake[5] not be aknowen[6]
what they know. For at the consecration of a bishop, every man

9. against.   1. valid.   2. fancy.
3. *made so strange:* treated as such a matter of surprise.
4. contrived.   5. *for ... sake:* for the sake of appearances.
6. *be aknowen:* acknowledge.

woteth well, by the paying for his bulls, that he purposeth to be one, and though he pay for nothing else.[7] And yet must he be twice asked whether he will be bishop or no, and he must twice say nay, and at the third time take it as compelled thereunto by his own will. And in a stage play all the people know right well that he that playeth the sowdaine[8] is percase a sowter.[9] Yet if one should can so little good[1] to show out of season[2] what acquaintance he hath with him and call him by his own name while he standeth in his majesty, one of his tormentors[3] might hap to break his head, and worthy,[4] for marring of the play. And so they said that these matters be kings' games, as it were, stage plays, and for the more part played upon scaffolds,[5] in which poor men be but the lookers-on. And they that wise be will meddle no farther. For they that sometime step up and play with them, when they cannot play their parts, they disorder the play and do themself no good.

The next day[6] the protector, with a great train, went to Westminster Hall[7] and there, when he had placed himself in the Court of the King's Bench,[8] declared to the audience that he would take upon him the crown in that place there, where the king himself sitteth and ministreth the law, because he considered that it was the chiefest duty of a king to minister the laws. Then, with as pleasant an oration as he could, he went about to win unto him the nobles, the merchants, the artificers, and, in conclusion, all kind of men, but specially the lawyers[9] of this realm. And finally, to the intent that no man should

7. *and ... else:* even though he has made no payment to the king for preferment.
8. sultan. 9. shoemaker. 1. *can ... good:* be so foolish as.
2. *out of season:* inopportunely. 3. official torturers [in the play?].
4. deservedly.
5. Both the stage upon which plays were performed and the platform erected for an execution.
6. June 26.
7. *Westminster Hall:* the hall at the palace of Westminster.
8. *Court ... Bench:* Seat of royal judgment where pleas are heard and judgments made in the name of the king.
9. Undoubtedly part of Richard's attempt to find legal sanction for his title.

hate him for fear and that his deceitful clemency might get
him the good will of the people, when he had declared the dis-
commodity[1] of discord and the commodities[2] of concord and
unity, he made an open proclamation that he did put out of
his mind all enmities and that he there did openly pardon all
offenses committed against him. And to the intent that he
might show a proof thereof, he commanded that one Fogge,[3]
whom he had long deadly hated, should be brought then before him. Who being brought out of the sanctuary by[4] (for
thither had he fled, for fear of him), in the sight of the people,
he took him by the hand. Which thing the common people rejoiced at and praised, but wise men took it for a vanity. In his
return homeward, whomsoever he met, he saluted. For a mind
that knoweth itself guilty is in a manner dejected[5] to a servile
flattery.

When he had begun his reign the twenty-sixth day of June,
after this mockish election, then was he crowned the sixth day
of July. And that solemnity was furnished for the most part
with the self same provision that was appointed for the coronation of his nephew.[6]

Now fell their mischief thick. And as the thing evil gotten is
never well kept, through all the time of his reign never ceased
there cruel death and slaughter, till his own destruction ended
it. But as he finished his time with the best death and the most
righteous, that is to wit his own, so began he with the most
piteous and wicked; I mean the lamentable murder of his innocent nephews, the young king and his tender brother, whose
death and final infortune[7] hath nevertheless so far comen in
question that some remain yet in doubt whether they were in
his days destroyed or no. Not for that only that Perkin War-

---

1. disadvantageousness.   2. material advantages.
3. Sir John Fogge (1425–90). Characterized as one of Edward IV's
"grasping favorites," he had been treasurer of the household from
1460 to 1469.
4. lying nearby.   5. humbled.
6. More's Latin text stops at this point.   7. misfortune.

beck,[8] by many folk's malice and more folk's folly so long space abusing the world, was as well with princes as the poorer people reputed and taken for the younger of those two; but for that also that all things were in late days so covertly demeaned,[9] one thing pretended and another meant, that there was nothing so plain and openly proved, but that yet for the common custom of close and covert dealing men had it ever inwardly suspect, as many well-counterfeited[1] jewels make the true mistrusted. Howbeit, concerning that opinion,[2] with the occasions moving either party, we shall have place more at large to entreat, if we hereafter happen to write the time of the late noble prince of famous memory, King Henry the Seventh, or percase that history of Perkin in any compendious process[3] by itself.

But in the meantime, for this present matter, I shall rehearse you the dolorous end of those babes, not after every way that I have heard, but after that way that I have so heard by such men and by such means as me thinketh it were hard but it should be true. King Richard, after his coronation, taking his way to Gloucester to visit in his new honor the town of which he bare the name of his old, devised, as he rode, to fulfill that thing which he before had intended. And forasmuch as his mind gave him that, his nephews living, men would not reckon that he could have right to the realm, he thought therefore without delay to rid[4] them, as though the killing of his kinsmen could amend his cause and make him a kindly[5] king.

Whereupon he sent one John Green,[6] whom he specially

---

8. Perkin Warbeck (d. 1499) famous pretender to the throne whose impersonation of the Duke of York deceived both James IV of Scotland and Maximilian, King of the Romans.
9. *covertly demeaned:* secretly managed.   1. imitated.
2. i.e., the opinion that the princes were still alive in the 1490s.
3. narrative. More apparently never wrote either of the planned histories.
4. get rid of.   5. proper.
6. A John Green had been a member of Edward IV's household as early as 1474–75.

trusted, unto Sir Robert Brackenbury,[7] Constable of the Tower, with a letter and credence also that the same Sir Robert should in any wise put the two children to death. This John Green did his errand unto Brackenbury, kneeling before Our Lady[8] in the Tower, who plainly answered that he would never put them to death, to die therefor;[9] with which answer John Green, returning, recounted the same to King Richard at Warwick,[1] yet in his way.[2]

Wherewith he took such displeasure and thought that the same night he said unto a secret[3] page of his: "Ah, whom shall a man trust? Those that I have brought up myself, those that I had went[4] would most surely serve me—even those fail me and at my command will do nothing for me."

"Sir," quod his page, "there lieth one on your pallet[5] without, that, I dare well say, to do your grace pleasure, the thing were right hard that he would refuse," meaning this by[6] Sir James Tyrell,[7] which was a man of right goodly personage and for nature's gifts worthy to have served a much better prince, if he had well served God and by grace obtained as much truth and good will as he had strength and wit. The man had an high[8] heart and sore longed upward, not rising yet so fast as he had hoped, being hindered and kept under by means of Sir Richard Radcliff and Sir William Catesby, which longing for no more partners of the prince's favor, and namely not for him whose pride they wist would bear no peer, kept him by secret drifts[9] out of all secret trust. Which thing this page well had

---

7. Sir Robert Brackenbury, appointed Constable of the Tower on July 17, 1483.

8. *Our Lady:* i.e., a statue of the virgin.

9. *to die therefor:* even if he should die for his refusal.

1. Richard was at Warwick from August 7 to August 15.

2. *yet . . . way:* while still on his progress.   3. intimate.

4. thought.   5. *on your pallet:* in your bedchamber.

6. *meaning this by:* referring to.

7. Sir James Tyrell (1445–1502), knighted in 1471, made knight banneret in 1482 for his services in the Scotch campaign. He was completely trusted by Richard.

8. proud.   9. schemes.

marked and known. Wherefore this occasion offered, of very special friendship he took his time to put him forward and by such wise do him good, that all the enemies he had except the devil could never have done him so much hurt.

For upon this page's words King Richard arose (for this communication had he sitting at the draught,[1] a convenient carpet for such a council) and came out into the pallet chamber, on which he found in bed Sir James and Sir Thomas Tyrell,[2] of person like and brethren of blood, but nothing of kin in conditions.[3] Then said the king merrily to them: "What, sirs, be ye in bed so soon?" and calling up Sir James brake[4] to him secretly his mind in this mischievous matter, in which he found him nothing strange.[5] Wherefore on the morrow he sent him to Brackenbury with a letter by which he was commanded to deliver Sir James all the keys of the Tower for one night, to the end he might there accomplish the king's pleasure in such thing as he had given him commandment. After which letter delivered and the keys received, Sir James appointed the night next ensuing to destroy them, devising before and preparing the means.

The prince, as soon as the protector left that name and took himself as king, had it showed unto him that he should not reign, but his uncle should have the crown. At which word the prince, sore abashed, began to sigh and said: "Alas! I would my uncle would let me have my life yet, though I lose my kingdom." Then he that told him the tale used him with good words and put him in the best comfort he could. But forthwith was the prince and his brother both shut up and all other removed from them, only one called Black Will or William Slaughter[6] except, set to serve them and see them sure.[7] After

1. privy.
2. Sir Thomas Tyrell (1450–1510) younger brother of James, knighted by Henry VII in 1487.
3. personal qualities.   4. revealed.   5. unwilling.
6. William Slaughter and the accused murderers Forest and Dighton all appear in contemporary records.
7. safe.

which time the prince never tied his points[8] nor ought rought[9] of himself, but with that young babe his brother lingered in thought and heaviness till this traitorous death delivered them of that wretchedness.

For Sir James Tyrell devised that they should be murdered in their beds, to the execution whereof he appointed Miles Forest, one of the four that kept them, a fellow fleshed[1] in murder before time. To him he joined one John Dighton, his own horsekeeper, a big, broad, square, strong knave. Then, all the other being removed from them, this Miles Forest and John Dighton about midnight (the sely[2] children lying in their beds) came into the chamber and suddenly lapped[3] them up among the clothes—so bewrapped them and entangled them, keeping down by force the featherbed and pillows hard unto their mouths, that within a while, smored[4] and stifled, their breath failing, they gave up to God their innocent souls into the joys of heaven, leaving to the tormentors their bodies dead in the bed. Which after that the wretches perceived, first by the struggling with the pains of death, and after long lying still, to be thoroughly dead, they laid their bodies naked out upon the bed and fetched Sir James to see them. Which, upon the sight of them, caused those murderers to bury them at the stair foot, meetly deep in the ground, under a great heap of stones.

Then rode Sir James in great haste to King Richard and showed him all the manner of the murder, who gave him great thanks and, as some say, there made him knight. But he allowed not, as I have heard, the burying in so vile a corner, saying that he would have them buried in a better place because they were a king's sons. Lo, the honorable courage[5] of a king! Whereupon they say that a priest of Sir Robert Brackenbury took up the bodies again and secretly interred them in such place as, by the occasion of his death which only knew it, could never since come to light. Very truth is it and well known that at such time as

8. laces for attaching hose to doublet.   9. took care.
1. initiated.   2. innocent.   3. wrapped.   4. smothered.
5. nature.

Sir James Tyrell was in the Tower for treason[6] committed against the most famous prince, King Henry the Seventh, both Dighton and he were examined and confessed the murder in manner above written, but whither the bodies were removed they could nothing tell.

And thus, as I have learned of them that much knew and little cause had to lie, were these two noble princes—these innocent, tender children, born of most royal blood, brought up in great wealth, likely long to live, to reign and rule in the realm —by traitorous tyranny taken, deprived of their estate,[7] shortly[8] shut up in prison, and privily slain and murdered; their bodies cast God wot where by the cruel ambition of their unnatural uncle and his dispiteous[9] tormentors. Which things on every part well pondered, God never gave this world a more notable example neither in what unsurety standeth this worldly weal,[1] or what mischief worketh the proud enterprise of a high heart, or finally, what wretched end ensueth such dispiteous cruelty.

For first to begin with the ministers:[2] Miles Forest at Saint Martin's[3] piecemeal rotted away. Dighton, indeed, yet walketh on alive in good possibility to be hanged ere he die. But Sir James Tyrell died at Tower Hill, beheaded for treason. King Richard himself, as ye shall hereafter hear, slain in the field, hacked and hewed of his enemies' hands, harried[4] on horseback dead, his hair in despite[5] torn and tugged like a cur dog. And the mischief that he took,[6] within less than three years of the mischief that he did; and yet all the meantime spent in much pain and trouble outward; much fear, anguish, and sorrow within. For I have heard by credible report of such as were secret with his chamberers that, after this abominable deed done, he never had quiet in his mind; he never thought himself sure. Where he went abroad, his eyes whirled about; his

6. Tyrell was executed on May 6, 1502, for his involvement in the conspiracy of Edmund de la Pole against Henry VII.
7. rank.   8. speedily.   9. pitiless.   1. state.
2. agents.   3. St. Martin le Grand, a sanctuary at Westminster.
4. dragged about.   5. *in despite:* contemptuously.   6. received.

body privily fenced,[7] his hand ever on his dagger, his countenance and manner like one always ready to strike again. He took ill rest a nights, lay long waking and musing, sore wearied with care and watch, rather slumbered than slept, troubled with fearful dreams, suddenly sometime start up, leap out of his bed and run about the chamber; so was his restless heart continually tossed and tumbled with the tedious impression and stormy remembrance of his abominable deed.

Now had he outward[8] no long time in rest. For hereupon soon after began the conspiracy,[9] or rather good confederation, between the Duke of Buckingham and many other gentlemen against him. The occasion whereupon the king and the duke fell out is of divers folk divers wise pretended.[1] This duke, as I have for certain been informed, as soon as the Duke of Gloucester, upon the death of King Edward, came to York and there had solemn funeral service for King Edward, sent thither in the most secret wise he could one Percival,[2] his trusty servant, who came to John Ward, a chamberer[3] of like secret trust with the Duke of Gloucester, desiring that in the most close and covert manner he might be admitted to the presence and speech of his master. And the Duke of Gloucester, advertised[4] of his desire, caused him in the dead of the night, after all other folk avoided,[5] to be brought unto him in his secret chamber, where Percival, after his master's recommendation, showed him that he had secretly sent him to show him that in this new world he would take such part as he would and wait upon him with a thousand good fellows if need were. The messenger, sent back with thanks and some secret instruction of the protector's mind, yet met him again with farther message from the duke, his master, within few days after at Nottingham, whither the protector from York, with many gentlemen of the north country

---

7. *privily fenced:* secretly shielded.   8. publicly.

9. Buckingham's revolt against Richard ended with his execution at Salisbury on November 2, 1483.

1. reported.   2. Probably Sir Humphrey Percival (d. 1498).

3. valet.   4. informed.   5. withdrew.

to the number of six hundred horse, was comen on his way to Londonward. And after secret meeting and communication had, eftsoon[6] departed.

Whereupon at Northampton the duke met with the protector himself with three hundred horses and from thence still continued with, partner of all his devises, till that after his coronation they departed, as it seemed, very great friends at Gloucester. From whence, as soon as the duke came home, he so lightly[7] turned from him and so highly conspired against him that a man would marvel whereof the change grew. And surely the occasion of their variance is of divers men diversely reported. Some have I heard say that the duke a little before the coronation, among other things, required of the protector the Duke of Hereford's lands,[8] to which he pretended himself just inheritor. And forasmuch as the title which he claimed by inheritance was somewhat interlaced with the title to the crown by the line of King Henry[9] before deprived, the protector conceived such indignation that he rejected the duke's request with many spiteful and minatory[1] words, which so wounded his heart with hatred and mistrust that he never after could endure to look aright on King Richard, but ever feared his own life, so far forth that when the protector rode through London toward his coronation, he feigned himself sick because he would not ride with him. And the other, taking it in evil part, sent him word to rise and come ride, or he would make him be carried. Whereupon he rode on with evil will and that notwithstanding, on the morrow rose from the feast, feigning himself sick; and King Richard said it was done in hatred and despite of him. And they say that ever after, continually, each of them lived in such hatred and distrust of other that the duke verily looked to

6. soon afterwards.   7. quickly.

8. The lands of Humphrey of Bohun, Duke of Hereford, belonged by right to Buckingham, since the Bohun line had become extinct with the death of Henry VI.

9. Henry IV, by marrying Mary Bohun, had established the throne's initial claim to the Hereford lands.

1. menacing.

have been murdered at Gloucester from which, nevertheless, he in fair manner departed.

But surely some right secret at the days[2] deny this; and many right wise men think it unlikely (the deep dissimuling[3] nature of those both men considered, and what need in that green world the protector had of the duke, and in what peril the duke stood if he fell once in suspicion of the tyrant) that either the protector would give the duke occasion of displeasure, or the duke the protector occasion of mistrust. And utterly[4] men think that if King Richard had any such opinion conceived, he would never have suffered him to escape his hands. Very truth it is, the duke was an high-minded man and evil[5] could bear the glory of another, so that I have heard of some that said they saw it that the duke, at such time as the crown was first set upon the protector's head, his eye could not abide the sight thereof, but wried[6] his head another way. But men say that he was of truth not well at ease, and that both to King Richard well known and not ill taken, nor any demand of the duke's uncourteously rejected, but he both with great gifts and high behests[7] in most loving and trusty manner departed at Gloucester.

But soon after his coming home to Brecknock,[8] having there in his custody, by the commandment of King Richard, Doctor Morton, Bishop of Ely, who, as ye before heard, was taken in the council at the Tower, waxed with him familiar, whose wisdom abused[9] his pride to his own deliverance and the duke's destruction. The bishop[1] was a man of great natural wit, very well learned, and honorable in behavior, lacking no wise ways to win favor. He had been fast[2] upon the part of King Henry

2. *some . . . days:* i.e., those who were privy to secret matters at that time.

3. dissembling.   4. indeed.   5. ill.   6. turned aside.

7. promises.   8. That is, to the duke's castle of Brecknock in Wales.

9. deceived.

1. For a similar portrait of Cardinal Morton, see the *Utopia* (*CW 4,* 58–60).

2. firm.

while that part was in wealth, and nevertheless left it not, nor
forsook it in woe: but fled the realm with the queen and the
prince, while King Edward had the king in prison, never came
home but to the field.[3] After which lost and that part utterly
subdued, the other,[4] for his fast faith and wisdom, not only
was content to receive him, but also wooed him to come and
had him from thenceforth both in secret trust and very special
favor, which he nothing deceived. For he being, as ye have
heard, after King Edward's death, first taken by the tyrant for
his truth[5] to the king, found the mean to set this duke in his
top;[6] joined gentlemen together in aid of King Henry, devising
first the marriage between him and King Edward's daughter,
by which his faith declared and good service to both his masters
at once, with infinite benefit to the realm by the conjunction of
those two bloods in one,[7] whose several[8] titles had long en-
quieted[9] the land. He fled the realm, went to Rome, never
minding more to meddle with the world till the noble prince,
King Henry the Seventh, gat[1] him home again, made him Archbishop of Canterbury and Chancellor of England, whereunto
the pope joined the honor of cardinal. Thus, living many days
in as much honor as one man might well wish, ended them so
godly that his death, with God's mercy, well changed his life.

This man, therefore, as I was about to tell you, by the long
and often alternate proof,[2] as well of prosperity as adverse
fortune, had gotten by great experience (the very mother and
mistress of wisdom), a deep insight in politic, worldly drifts;
whereby, perceiving now this duke glad to comen[3] with him,
fed him with fair words and pleasant praises. And perceiving
by the process[4] of their communications the duke's pride now
and then balk out[5] a little breide[6] of envy toward the glory of

3. i.e., the Battle of Tewkesbury.   4. Edward IV.
5. loyalty.   6. *set . . . top:* bring things down on his ears.
7. *conjunction . . . one:* the marriage of Henry VII and Elizabeth of
York in 1486 united the houses of Lancaster and York and brought
an end to the Wars of the Roses.
8. separate.   9. disquieted.   1. got.   2. experience.
3. confer.   4. course.   5. *balk out:* give vent to.   6. outburst.

the king, and thereby feeling him ethe[7] to fall out if the matter were well handled, he craftily sought the ways to prick him forward,[8] taking always the occasion of his coming, and so keeping himself close within his bonds that he rather seemed to follow him than to lead him.

For when the duke first began to praise and boast[9] the king and show how much profit the realm should take by his reign, my Lord Morton answered: "Surely, my lord, folly were it for me to lie, for if I would swear the contrary, your lordship would not, I ween, believe, but that if the world would have gone as I would have wished, King Henry's son[1] had had the crown and not King Edward. But after that God had ordered him to lose it and King Edward to reign, I was never so mad that I would with a dead man strive against the quick.[2] So was I to King Edward faithful chaplain and glad would have been that his child had succeeded him. Howbeit, if the secret judgment of God have otherwise provided, I purpose not to spurn against a prick,[3] nor labor to set up that God pulleth down. And as for the late protector and now king. . . "

And even there he left,[4] saying that he had already meddled too much with the world and would fro that day meddle with his book and his beads[5] and no further. Then longed the duke sore to hear what he would have said because he ended with the king and there so suddenly stopped, and exhorted him so familiarly between them twain to be bold to say whatsoever he thought; whereof he faithfully promised there should never come hurt and peradventure more good than he would ween, and that himself intended to use his faithful, secret advice and counsel which, he said, was the only cause for which he procured[6] of the king to have him in his custody where he might reckon himself at home, and else had he been put in the hands of them with whom he should not have found the like favor.

7. easy.   8. *prick him forward:* incite him.   9. extol.
1. Prince Edward, son of Henry VI.   2. living.
3. *spurn . . . prick:* rebel against a spur.   4. stopped speaking.
5. *book . . . beads:* breviary and rosary.   6. obtained permission.

The bishop right humbly thanked him and said: "In good faith, my lord, I love not much to talk much of princes, as thing not all out of peril, though the word be without fault—forasmuch as it shall not be taken as the party meant it, but as it pleaseth the prince to conster[7] it. And ever I think on Aesop's tale, that when the lion had proclaimed that on pain of death there should none horned beast abide in that wood, one that had in his forehead a bunch[8] of flesh fled away a great pace.[9] The fox that saw him run so fast asked him whither he made all that haste. And he answered: 'In faith, I neither wot nor reck,[1] so I were once hence because of this proclamation made of horned beasts.'

" 'What, fool!' quod the fox. 'Thou mayest abide well enough; the lion meant not by thee, for it is none horn that is in thine head.'

" 'No, marry,' quod he, 'that wot I well enough. But what and he call it an horn, where am I then?' "

The duke laughed merrily at the tale and said: "My lord, I warrant you, neither the lion nor the boar[2] shall pick any matter at[3] any thing here spoken, for it shall never come near their ear."

"In good faith, sir," said the bishop, "if it did, the thing that I was about to say, taken as well as afore God I meant it, could deserve but thank. And yet taken as I ween it would, might happen to turn me to little good and you to less."

Then longed the duke yet much more to wit[4] what it was. Whereupon the bishop said: "In good faith, my lord, as for the late protector, sith[5] he is now king in possession, I purpose not to dispute his title. But for the weal of this realm whereof his grace hath now the governance and whereof I am myself one poor member, I was about to wish that to those good abilities, whereof he hath already right many little needing my praise, it

---

7. construe. 8. lump. 9. *a great pace:* at a great speed.
1. *wot nor reck:* know nor care.
2. *lion . . . boar:* The lion and the boar formed the royal arms of Richard III.
3. *pick . . at:* find fault with. 4. know. 5. since.

might yet have pleased God for the better store[6] to have given him some of such other excellent virtues meet for the rule of a realm, as our Lord hath planted in the person of your grace."

6. provision.

SELECTIONS
FROM
THE ENGLISH POEMS

A mery gest
how a sergeaunt wolde
lerne to be a frere

Wyse men alwaye,
Afferme & say,
    That best is for a man:
Dylygently,
For to apply,   5
    The besynes that he can,
And in no wyse,
To enterpryse,
    An other faculte,
For he that wyll,   10
And can no skyll,
    Is neuer lyke to the.
He that hath lafte,
The hosiers crafte,
    & falleth to makynge shone,   15
The smythe that shall,
To payntynge fall,
    His thryfte is wel nygh done.
A blacke draper,
With wyte paper,   20
    To go to wrytynge scole,
An olde butler,
Becum a cutler,
    I wene shal prove a fole.
An olde trot,   25

6. *besynes:* business, occupation.   7. *wyse:* way.
9. *faculte:* trade, skill.   11. *can no skyll:* has no knowledge.
12. *the:* prosper.   13. *lafte:* left.   15. *shone:* shoes.
18. *thryfte:* prosperity.
24. *wene . . . prove:* think shall turn out to be.   25. *trot:* hag.

99

That good can not,
    But ever kysse the cup,
With her physyke,
Wyll kepe one seke,
    Tyll she have soused hym up.   30
A man of lawe,
That never sawe,
    The wayes to by and sell,
Wenynge to aryse,
By marchaundyse,   35
    I praye god spede hym well.
A marchaunt eke,
That wyll good seke,
    By all the meanes he maye,
To fall in sute,   40
Tyll he dyspute,
    His monay clene awaye,
Pletynge the lawe,
For every strawe,
    Shall prove a thryfty man,   45
With bate and stryfe,
But by my lyfe,
    I can not tell you whan.
Whan an hatter
Wyll go smater,   50
    In phylosophy,
Or a pedlar,
Waxe a medlar,
    In theology,
All that ensewe,   55

26–27. *That . . . cup:* i.e., the only thing she does well is to kiss the (drinking) cup.
28. *physyke:* medicine.   29. *seke:* sick.   33. *by:* buy.
34. *Wenynge:* Thinking.   37. *eke:* too.   38. *seke:* seek.
40. *sute:* a lawsuit.   43. *Pletynge:* Pleading.
46. *bate:* argument.   55. *ensewe:* follow.

Suche craftes newe,
    They dryve so fere a cast,
That evermore,
They do therefore,
    Beshrewe themselfe at laste.   60
This thynge was tryed
And verefyed,
    Here by a sergeaunt late,
That ryfely was,
Or he coude pas,   65
    Rapped aboute the pate,
Whyle that he wolde
Se how he coude,
    In goddes name play the frere:
Now yf you wyll,   70
Knowe how hyt fyll,
    Take hede & ye shall here.
It happed so,
Not longe ago,
    A thryfty man dyede,   75
An hondred pounde,
Of nobles rounde,
    That had he layde a syde:
His sone he wolde,
Sholde have this golde,   80
    For to begyne with all:
But to suffyce
His chylde, well thryes,
    That monay were to small.
Yet or this daye   85

---

57. *dryve . . . cast:* are so far off the mark.
63. *sergeaunt:* a sergeant of the law.
64. *ryfely:* frequently, abundantly.   65. *Or:* Before; *pas:* escape.
69. *frere:* friar.   71. *hyt fyll:* it happened.
77. *nobles:* gold coins worth, in More's day, about 10s.
83. *thryes:* thrice.   85. *or:* before.

I have herde saye,
    That many a man certesse,
Hath with good cast,
Be ryche at last,
    That hath begon with lesse.   90
But this yonge man,
So well began,
    His monaye to imploye,
That certenly,
His policy,   95
    To se hyt was a joye.
For lest sum blaste,
Myght over caste,
    His shyp, or by myschaunce,
Men with some wyle,   100
Myght hym begyle,
    And mynysshe his substaunce,
For to put out,
All manere doubte,
    He made a good purvaye   105
For every whyt,
By his owne wyt,
    And toke an other waye:
Fyrste fayre and wele,
Therof grete dele,   110
    He dyghth yt in a pot,
But then hym thought,
That way was nought,
    And there he lefte hyt not.
So was he fayne,   115

87. *certesse:* to be sure.   88. *cast:* management.
89. *Be:* Become.
102. *mynysshe his substaunce:* diminish his capital.
104. *manere:* kind of.   105. *purvaye:* arrangement.
106. *whyt:* bit.   109. *wele:* well.   110. *dele:* deal.
111. *dyghth:* put.

Frome thens agayne,
   To put hyt in a cup,
And by and by,
Covetously,
   He supped hyt fayre up.   120
In his owne brest,
He thought hyt best,
   His monaye to enclose,
Then wyst he well,
What ever fell,   125
   He coude hyt never lose.
He borowed than,
Of another man,
   Monaye and marchaundyse:
Never payde hyt,   130
Up he layde hyt,
   In lyke maner wyse.
Yet on the gere,
That he wolde were,
   He rought not what he spente,   135
So hyt were nyce,
As for the pryce,
   Coude hym not myscontente.
With lusty sporte,
And with resorte,   140
   Of joly company,
In myrthe and playe,
Full many a daye,
   He lyved merely.
And men had sworne,   145
Some man is borne,
   To have a goodly floure,

133. *gere:* clothing.   135. *rought:* cared.
136–38. *So . . . myscontente:* As long as it appealed to him, he was never discontented with the price.
144. *merely:* merrily.   147. *floure:* flowering.

And so was he,
For suche degre,
 He gate and suche honoure,   150
That with out doubte,
When he went out,
 A sergaunt well and fayre,
Was redy strayte,
On him to wayte,   155
 As sowne as on the mayre.
But he doubtlesse,
Of his mekenes,
 Hated suche pompe & pryde,
And wolde not go,   160
Companyed so,
 But drewe hym selfe a syde,
To saynt Katheryne,
Streyght as a lyne,
 He gate hym at a tyde,   165
For devocion,
Or promocyon,
 There wolde he nedes abyde.
There spente he fast,
Tyll all was past,   170
 And to hym came there many,
To aske theyr det,
But non coude get,
 The valour of a peny.
With vysage stoute,   175
He bare hyt oute,
 Even unto the harde hedge,

149. *degre:* a position in society. 150. *gate:* got.
163. *saynt Katheryne:* the convent and hospital of St. Katherine, a well-known sanctuary for thieves and debtors.
165. *tyde:* certain time.
167. *promocyon:* i.e., because he feared that someone might inform on him if he did not make use of the protection of the hospital.
174. *valour:* value. 177. *Even . . . hedge:* Right to the very limit.

A moneth or twayne,
Tyll he was fayne,
   To laye his gowne to pledge.   180
Than was he there,
In greter fere,
   Then or that he came thyder,
And wolde as fayne,
Departe agayne,   185
   But that he wyst not whyther.
Than after this,
To a frende of his,
   He went and there abode,
Where as he laye,   190
So syke al waye,
   He myght not come abrode.
Hyt happed than,
A marchaunt man,
   That he ought monaye to,   195
Of an offycere,
Than gan enquyre,
   What hym was best to do.
And he answerde,
Be not a ferde,   200
   Take an accyon therfore,
I you beheste,
I shall hym reste,
   And than care for no more.
I fere quod he,   205
Hyt wyll not be,
   For he wyll not com out.
The sergeaunt sayd,
Be not afrayde,
   Hyt shall be brought aboute.   210

183. *or:* before; *thyder:* thither.   195. *ought:* owed.
197. *gan:* began to.   200. *a ferde:* afraid.
202. *beheste:* promise.   203. *reste:* arrest.

In many a game,
Lyke to the same,
   Have I bene well in ure,
And for your sake,
Let me be bake,   215
   But yf I do this cure.
Thus part they bothe,
And to hym goth,
   A pace this offycere,
And for a daye,   220
All his araye,
   He chaunged with a frere.
So was he dyght,
That no man myght,
   Hym for a frere deny,   225
He dopped and doked,
He spake and loked,
   So relygyously.
Yet in a glasse,
Or he wolde passe,   230
   He toted and he pered,
His herte for pryde,
Lepte in his syde,
   To se how well he frered.
Than forth a pace,   235
Unto the place,
   He goeth in goddes name,
To do this dede,
But nowe take hede,

213. *in ure:* experienced.   215. *bake:* baked.
216. *But . . . cure:* If I don't bring this matter off successfully.
219. *A pace:* Quickly.
223. *dyght:* dressed.
226. *dopped and doked:* bowed his head and cringed.
231. *toted:* gazed; *pered:* peered.
234. *frered:* played the part of a friar.

For here begynneth the game.   240
He drewe hym nye,
And softely,
    At the dore he knocked:
A damoysell,
That herde hym well,   245
    Came & it unlocked.
The frere sayd,
God spede fayre mayde,
    Here lodgeth such a man,
It is tolde me: 250
Well syr quod she,
    And yf he do what than?
Quod he maystresse,
No harme doubtlesse:
    Hyt longethe for our ordre,   255
To hurte no man,
But as we can,
    Every wyght to fordre:
With hym truely,
Fayne speke wolde I.   260
    Syr quod she by my faye,
He is so syke,
Ye be not lyke,
    To speke with hym to daye.
Quod he fayre maye,   265
Yet I you praye,
    This moche at my desyre,
Vouchesafe to do,
As go hym to,
    And saye an austen frere,   270
Wolde with hym speke,

255. *Hyt . . . for:* It is the duty of.
258. *wyght to fordre:* creature to help.
261. *faye:* faith.   265. *maye:* maiden.
270. *austen:* Augustinian.

And maters breke,
   For his avayle certyne.
Quod she I wyll,
Stonde ye here styll,   275
   Tyll I come downe agayne.
Up is she go.
And tolde hym so,
   As she was bode to saye,
He mystrystynge,   280
No maner thynge,
   Sayd mayden go thy waye,
And fetche hym hyder,
That we togyder,
   May talke. Adowne she goth,   285
Up she hym brought,
No harme she thought,
   But it made some folke wroth.
But this offycere,
This fayned frere,   290
   Whan he was come alofte,
He dopped than,
And grete this man,
   Relygyously and ofte.
And he agayne,   295
Ryght gladde & fayne,
   Toke hym there by the honde,
The frere than sayd,
Ye be dysmayde,
   With trouble I understonde.   300
In dede quod he,
Hyt hath with me,

272. *breke:* discuss.
273. *For ... certyne:* which will assuredly help him.
279. *bode:* bidden.   280. *mystrystynge:* suspecting.
281. *No ... thynge:* nothing at all.   288. *wroth:* angry.
292. *dopped:* bowed.   293. *grete:* greeted.

Ben better than hyt is.
Syr quod the frere,
Be of good chere,   305
    Yet shall hyt after this,
For crystes sake,
Loke that you take,
    No thought within your brest:
God may tourne all,   310
And so he shall,
    I truste unto the best.
But I wolde now,
Comyn with you,
    In counsell yf you please,   315
Or elles nat,
Of maters that,
    Shall set your herte at ease.
Downe went the mayde,
The marchaunt sayd,   320
    Now say on gentyll frere,
Of all this tydynge,
That ye me brynge,
    I longe full sore to here.
Whan there was none,   325
But they alone,
    The frere with evyll grace,
Sayd I rest the,
Come on with me,
    And out he toke his mace: 330
Thou shalte obaye,
Come on thy waye,
    I have the in my cloche,
Thou goest not hense,

314. *Comyn:* Talk.   315. *In counsell:* In private.
316. *Or elles nat:* "If you don't want to, we won't."
327. *evyll:* ill.   328. *rest the:* arrest thee.
330. *mace:* symbol of his office as sergeant.   333. *cloche:* clutch.

For all the pense,   335
    The mayre hath in his pouche.
This marchaunt there,
For wrathe and fere,
    Waxed welnyghe wode,
Sayde horsone thefe,   340
With a mischefe,
    Who hath taught the thy good?
And with his fyste,
Upon the lyste,
    He gave hym suche a blowe,   345
That bacwarde downe,
Almoste in sowne,
    The frere is overthrowe.
Yet was this man,
Well ferder than,   350
    Lest he the frere had slayne,
Tyll with good rappes,
And hevy clappes,
    He dawde hym up agayne.
The frere toke herte,   355
And up he sterte,
    And well he layed aboute,
And so there goth,
Betwene them bothe,
    Many a lusty cloute.   360
They rente and tere,
Eche other here,
    And clave togyder fast,
Tyll with luggynge,

339. *wode:* mad.   340. *horsone:* whoreson.
341. *mischefe:* curse upon you.
342. *Who . . . good?:* Who's taught you what was good for you?
344. *lyste:* cheek.   347. *in sowne:* knocked out.
350. *Well . . . than:* Very much afraid then.
354. *dawde hym up:* brought him to.
362. *other here:* others' hair.

Halynge & tugynge,   365
   They fell doune both at last.
Than on the grounde,
Togyder rounde,
   With many a sadde stroke,
They roll and rumble,   370
They tourne & tumble,
   Lyke pygges in a poke.
So longe above,
They heve and shove,
   Togyder that at the last,   375
The mayde and wyfe,
To breke the stryfe,
   Hyed them upwarde faste.
And whan they spye,
The captaynes lye,   380
   Waltrynge on the place,
The freres hode
They pulled a good,
   Adoune aboute his face.
Whyle he was blynde,   385
The wenche behynde,
   Lent hym on the flore,
Many a jolle,
Aboute the nolle,
   With a grete batylldore.   390
The wyfe came yet,
And with her fete,
   She holpe to kepe hym downe,
And with her rocke,

---

365. *Halynge:* Dragging.   369. *sadde:* heavy.
372. *poke:* bag.   381. *Waltrynge:* Rolling about.
382. *hode:* hood.   388. *jolle:* knock.   389. *nolle:* head.
390. *batylldore:* a wooden bat used for smoothing out clothes after
they had been washed.
392. *fete:* feet.   393. *holpe:* helped.   394. *rocke:* distaff.

Many a knocke,   395
   She gave hym on the crowne.
They layde his mace,
Aboute his face,
   That he was wode for payne,
The frere frappe,   400
Gate many a swappe,
   Tyll he was full nyghe slayne.
Up they hym lyfte,
And with evyll thryfte,
   Hedlynge all the stayre,   405
Downe they hym threwe,
And sayd a dewe,
   Commaunde us to the mayre.
The frere arose,
But I suppose,   410
   Amased was his hede,
He shoke his eres,
And from grete feres,
   He thought hym well a flede.
Quod he now lost,   415
Is all this cost,
   We be never the nere.
Ill mote he the,
That caused me,
   To make my selfe a frere.   420
Now maysters all,
And now I shall,
   Ende there I began,
In ony wyse,
I wolde avyse,   425

---

400. *frere frappe:* friar manqué, fake friar.
404. *with . . . thryfte:* to his bad luck.   405. *Hedlynge:* Headlong.
407. *a dewe:* adieu.   408. *Commaunde:* Commend.
411. *Amased:* Dazed.   415. *Quod:* Said.   417. *nere:* nearer.
418. *Ill . . . the:* May he never prosper.

And counseyll every man,
His owne craft use,
All newe refuse,
    And utterly let them gone:
Playe not the frere,   430
Now make good chere,
    And welcome everychone.

---

432. *everychone:* everyone. More's "Merry Jest" may well have been designed for recitation at a civic feast.

PAGEANT VERSES

Mayster Thomas More in his youth devysed in hys fathers house in London, a goodly hangyng of fyne paynted clothe, with nyne pageauntes, and verses over every of those pageauntes: which verses expressed and declared, what the ymages in those pageauntes represented: and also in those   5
pageauntes were paynted, the thynges that the verses over them dyd (in effecte) declare, whiche verses here folowe.

In the first pageant was painted a boy playing at the top & squyrge. And over this pageaunt was writen as foloweth.

Chyldhod   10

I am called Chyldhod, in play is all my mynde,
To cast a coyte, a cokstele, and a ball.
A toppe can I set, and dryve it in his kynde.
But would to god these hatefull bookes all,
Were in a fyre brent to pouder small.   15
Than myght I lede my lyfe alwayes in play:
Whiche lyfe god sende me to myne endyng day.

In the second pageaunt was paynted a goodly freshe yonge man, rydyng uppon a goodly horse, havynge an hawke on his fyste, and a brase of grayhowndes folowyng   20

---

2. *hangyng:* a wall hanging, designed both to prevent drafts and for ornamentation.
3. *pageauntes:* pictorial representations; *every:* each.
9. *squyrge:* whip, used to make the top spin.
12. *coyte:* quoit; *cokstele:* a stick to throw at a cock. The game was called "cockshying."
13. *dryve . . . kynde:* make it spin as it is supposed to do.
15. *brent:* burned; *pouder:* powder, ashes.   20. *brase:* brace.

hym. And under the horse fete, was paynted the same boy,
that in the fyrst pageaunte was playinge at the top &
squyrge. And over this second pageant the wrytyng was
thus.

Manhod   25

Manhod I am therefore I me delyght,
To hunt and hawke, to nourishe up and fede,
The grayhounde to the course, the hawke to the flyght,
And to bestryde a good and lusty stede.
These thynges become a very man in dede,   30
Yet thynketh this boy his pevishe game swetter,
But what no force, his reason is no better.

In the thyrd pagiaunt, was paynted the goodly younge
man in the seconde pagiaunt, lyeng on the grounde. And
uppon hym stode ladye Venus goddes of love, and by her   35
uppon this man stode the lytle god Cupyde. And over this
thyrd pageaunt, this was the wrytyng that foloweth.

Venus and Cupyde

Whoso ne knoweth the strength, power and myght,
Of Venus and me her lytle sonne Cupyde,   40
Thou Manhod shalt a myrour bene a ryght,
By us subdued for all thy great pryde,
My fyry dart perceth thy tender syde,
Now thou whiche erst despysedst children small,
Shall waxe a chylde agayne and be my thrall.   45

In the fourth pageaunt was paynted an olde sage father
sittyng in a chayre. And lyeng under his fete was painted
the ymage of Venus & Cupyde, that were in the third

21. *horse fete:* horse's feet.   28. *course:* pursuit of the quarry.
29. *stede:* steed.   30. *very:* true.   31. *swetter:* sweeter.
32. *force:* matter.   44. *erst:* formerly.

pageant. And over this fourth pageant the scripture was
thus.   50

Age

Olde Age am I, with lokkes, thynne and hore,
Of our short lyfe, the last and best part.
Wyse and discrete: the publike wele therefore,
I help to rule to my labour and smart,   55
Therefore Cupyde withdrawe thy fyry dart,
Chargeable matters shall of love oppresse,
Thy childish game and ydle bysinesse.

In the fyfth pageaunt was paynted an ymage of Death:
and under hys fete lay the olde man in the fourth pag-   60
eaunte. And above this fift pageant, this was the saying.

Deth

Though I be foule, ugly, lene and mysshape,
Yet there is none in all this worlde wyde,
That may my power withstande or escape.   65
Therefore sage father greatly magnifyed,
Discende from your chayre, set a part your pryde,
Witsafe to lende (though it be to your payne)
To me a fole, some of your wise brayne.

In the sixt pageant was painted lady Fame. And under   70
her fete was the picture of Death that was in the fifth
pageant. And over this sixt pageaunt the writyng was as
foloweth.

49. *scripture:* inscription.
52. *lokkes:* locks (of hair) ; *hore:* hoar, gray.   54. *wele:* weal.
57. *Chargeable:* Responsible; *of love:* to be construed with "game"
in the next line.
59. *ymage of Death:* i.e., a skull, or possibly a skeleton.
63. *lene and mysshape:* lean and misshapen.
66. *magnifyed:* extolled.   68. *Witsafe:* Vouchsafe.

Fame

Fame I am called, marvayle you nothing,   75
Though with tonges I am compassed all rounde
For in voyce of people is my chiefe livyng.
O cruel death, thy power I confounde.
When thou a noble man hast brought to grounde
Maugry thy teeth to lyve cause hym shall I,   80
Of people in parpetuall memory.

In the seventh pageant was painted the ymage of Tyme,
and under hys fete was lyeng the picture of Fame that was
in the sixt pageant. And this was the scripture over this
seventh pageaunt.   85

Tyme

I whom thou seest with horyloge in hande,
Am named tyme, the lord of every howre,
I shall in space destroy both see and lande.
O simple fame, how darest thou man honowre,   90
Promising of his name, an endlesse flowre,
Who may in the world have a name eternall,
When I shall in proces distroy the world and all.

In the eyght pageant was pictured the ymage of lady
Eternitee, sittyng in a chayre under a sumptious clothe of   95
estate, crowned with an imperial crown. And under her
fete lay the picture of Time, that was in the seventh pageant. And above this eight pageaunt, was it writen as
foloweth.

76. *compassed:* encircled.
80. *Maugry thy teeth:* In spite of anything you can do.
87. *horyloge:* hourglass.   91. *flowre:* flowering.
93. *proces:* due course.
95–96. *clothe of estate:* canopy placed over a royal seat.

Eternitee   100

Me nedeth not to bost, I am Eternitee,
The very name signifyeth well,
That myne empyre infinite shalbe.
Thou mortall Tyme every man can tell,
Art nothyng els but the mobilite   105
Of sonne and mone chaungyng in every degre;
When they shall leve theyr course thou shalt be brought,
For all thy pride and bostyng into nought.

In the nynth pageant was painted a Poet sitting in a
chayre. And over this pageant were there writen these   110
verses in latin folowyng.

The Poet

Has fictas quemcunque juvat spectare figuras,
    Sed mira veros quas putat arte homines,
Ille potest veris, animum sic pascere rebus,   115
    Ut pictis oculos pascit imaginibus.
Namque videbit uti fragilis bona lubrica mundi,
    Tam cito non veniunt, quam cito pretereunt,
Gaudia, laus & honor, celeri pede omnia cedunt,
    Qui manet excepto semper amore dei.   120
Ergo homines, levibus jamjam diffidite rebus,
    Nulla recessuro spes adhibenda bono,
Qui dabit eternam nobis pro munere vitam,
    In permansuro ponite vota deo.

113–24. More's Latin verses are translated as follows by L. Bradner
and C. A. Lynch (*The Latin Epigrams of Thomas More,* Chicago,
1953, p. 238): "If anyone finds pleasure in looking at these pictures
because he feels that, although they are products of the imagination,
still they represent man truly and with remarkable skill, then he can
delight his soul with the actual truth just as he feasts his eyes on its
painted image. For he will see that the elusive goods of this perishable
world do not come so readily as they pass away. Pleasures, praise,
homage, all things quickly disappear—except the love of God, which

A Rueful Lamentation

A ruful lamentacion (writen by master Thomas More in his youth) of the deth of quene Elisabeth mother to king Henry the eight, wife to king Henry the seventh, & eldest doughter to king Edward the fourth, which quene Elisabeth dyed in childbed in February in the yere of our lord .1503. & in the 18. yere of the raigne of king Henry the seventh.

O ye that put your trust and confidence,
In worldly joy and frayle prosperite,
That so lyve here as ye should never hence,
Remember death and loke here uppon me.
Ensaumple I thynke there may no better be.   5
Your selfe wotte well that in this realme was I,
Your quene but late, and lo now here I lye.

Was I not borne of olde worthy linage?
Was not my mother queene my father kyng?
Was I not a kinges fere in marriage?   10
Had I not plenty of every pleasaunt thyng?
Mercifull god this is a straunge reckenying:
Rychesse, honour, welth, and auncestry
Hath me forsaken and lo now here I ly.

If worship myght have kept me, I had not gone.   15
If wyt myght have me saved, I neded not fere.
If money myght have holpe, I lacked none.

---

endures forever. Therefore, mortals, put no confidence hereafter in trivialities, no hope in transitory advantage; offer your prayers to the everlasting God, who will grant us the gift of eternal life."

5. *Ensaumple:* Example.   6. *wotte:* know.

9. *mother:* Elizabeth Woodville, Edward IV's queen.

10. *fere:* consort, spouse.   13. *Rychesse:* Wealth (riches).

But O good God what vayleth all this gere?
When deth is come thy mighty messangere,
Obey we must, there is no remedy,   20
Me hath he sommoned, and lo now here I ly.

Yet was I late promised otherwyse,
This yere to live in welth and delice.
Lo where to commeth thy blandishyng promyse,
O false astrolagy and devynatrice,   25
Of goddes secretes makyng thy selfe so wyse.
How true is for this yere thy prophecy.
The yere yet lasteth, and lo nowe here I ly.

O bryttill welth, ay full of bitternesse,
Thy single pleasure doubled is with payne.   30
Account my sorow first and my distresse,
In sondry wyse, and recken there agayne
The joy that I have had, and I dare sayne,
For all my honour, endured yet have I,
More wo then welth, and lo now here I ly.   35

Where are our Castels, now where are our Towers,
Goodly Rychmonde sone art thou gone from me,
At westminster that costly worke of yours,

18. *vayleth . . . gere:* use are all these possessions.
23. *welth and delice:* happiness and delight.
25. *astrolagy and devynatrice:* astrology and divination. A court astrol-
oger, William Parron, who published various prophecies between 1498
and 1503, had predicted on New Year's Day, 1503, that the queen
would live to be eighty. She died on February 11 of that year at the
age of thirty-seven.
29. *ay:* ever.   31. *Account:* Add up.
32: *sondry wyse:* various ways.
36. *Where are . . . :* More echoes the *ubi sunt* theme that ran through
medieval literature.
37. *Rychmonde:* this royal palace was new at the time of the queen's
death.
38. *westminster:* Henry VII's royal chapel was then being built. The
queen was buried there after its completion.

Myne owne dere lorde, now shall I never see.
Almighty god vouchesafe to graunt that ye,   40
For you and your children well may edefy.
My palyce bylded is, and lo now here I ly.

Adew myne owne dere spouse, my worthy lorde,
The faithfull love that dyd us both combyne,
In mariage and peasable concorde,   45
Into your handes here I cleane resyne,
To be bestowed uppon your children and myne.
Erst wer you father, & now must ye supply,
The mothers part also, for lo now here I ly.

Farewell my doughter lady Margarete,   50
God wotte full oft it greved hath my mynde,
That ye should go where we should seldome mete.
Now am I gone, and have left you behynde.
O mortall folke that we be very blynde.
That we least feare, full oft it is most nye,   55
From you depart I fyrst, and lo now here I lye.

Farewell Madame my lordes worthy mother,
Comfort your sonne, and be ye of good chere.
Take all a worth, for it will be no nother.
Farewell my doughter Katherine late the fere,   60
To prince Arthur myne owne chyld so dere,

41. *edefy:* build.   42. *My palyce:* i.e., the grave.
45. *peasable:* peaceful.   48. *Erst:* Before (my death).
50. *Margarete:* the queen's second child (1489–1541). She married
James IV of Scotland on August 8, 1503. The queen alludes to her
coming marriage in line 52.
54. *that ... blynde:* how very blind we are.
57. *Madame:* Margaret Beaufort (1441–1509), Countess of Richmond
and Derby, Henry VII's mother.
59. *a worth:* in good part; *nother:* other.
60. *Katherine:* Catherine of Aragon (1485–1536), who had married
Prince Arthur (1486–1502) on November 14, 1501. Arthur died
shortly after the marriage.

It booteth not for me to wepe or cry,
Pray for my soule, for lo now here I ly.

Adew lord Henry my loving sonne adew.
Our lorde encrease your honour and estate,   65
Adew my doughter Mary bright of hew.
God make you vertuous, wyse and fortunate.
Adew swete hart my litle doughter Kate,
Thou shalt swete babe suche is thy desteny,
Thy mother never know, for lo now here I ly.   70

Lady Cicyly, Anne and Katheryne.
Farewell my welbeloved sisters three,
O lady Briget other sister myne,
Lo here the ende of worldly vanitee.
Now well are ye that earthly foly flee,   75
And hevenly thynges love and magnify,
Farewell and pray for me, for lo now here I ly.

Adew my lordes, adew my ladies all,
Adew my faithfull servauntes every chone,
Adew my commons whom I never shall,   80
See in this world, wherfore to the alone,
Immortall god verely three and one,
I me commende, thy infinite mercy,
Shew to thy servant, for lo now here I ly.

---

62. *booteth:* helps.   64. *Henry:* Henry VIII (1491–1547).
66. *Mary:* third daughter of Elizabeth (1496–1533). She married
Louis XII of France in 1514 and, after his death in 1515, Charles
Brandon, Duke of Suffolk. *hew:* complexion.
68. *Kate:* Elizabeth's seventh and last child, born February 2, 1503.
She died shortly after her mother's death.
71–73: *Cicyly ... Briget:* Elizabeth's four sisters: Cecily (1469–1507),
Anne (1475–1511), Catherine (1479–1527), and Bridget (1480–
1517); Bridget was a Dominican nun (cf. line 75).
76. *magnify:* praise.   79. *every chone:* every one of you.
80. *commons:* the people of England.
82. *verely:* truly.

Lewis the Lost Lover[1]

Ey[2] flatering fortune, loke thou never so fayre,
Or never so plesantly begin to smile,
As though thou wouldst my ruine all repayre,
During my life thou shalt me not begile.
Trust shall I god, to entre in a while
Hys haven of heaven sure and uniforme;
Ever after thy calme, loke I for a storme.

Davey the Dicer

Long was I lady Lucke your serving man,
And now have lost agayne all that I gat,[3]
Wherfore whan I thinke on you nowe and than,
And in my mynde remember this and that,
Ye may not blame me though I beshrew your cat,[4]
But in fayth I blesse you agayne a thousand times,
For lending me now some laysure to make rymes.

1. This and the following poem were first printed in More's *English Works* of 1557. The editor (p. 1432) says that More "made them for his pastime while he was prisoner in the Tower of London" (April 1534–July 1535).
2. Ah.
3. got.
4. *beshrew your cat:* i.e., curse whatever plans you may have made for me. "To turn the cat in the pan" was a dicing term which meant "to reverse the order of things so dexterously as to make them appear the opposite of what they really were."

SELECTIONS
FROM THE
LATIN POEMS

Rhenanus' Preface to the
March 1518 Edition of
More's Epigrams

Beatus Rhenanus[1] Greets Willibald
Pirckheimer,[2] Councilor to the
Emperor Maximilian and Mem-
ber of the Nuremberg Senate

It seemed quite agreeable and proper, most renowned Willibald,
for me to address specifically to you what our friend Erasmus of
Rotterdam recently sent to me, the *Epigrams* of Thomas More,
that ornament of Britain, since you and he are so alike in many
respects. You are both skilled in the law, both learned in Greek
as well as Latin. Not only are you both occupied in the public
duties of your respective states, but, because of your unusual skill
in resolving problems and your wisdom in council, you are both
very dear to your rulers, the one to the very powerful King
Henry of England, the other to the most holy Emperor Maximilian. Why mention wealth, which you both have in great
plenty, so that neither of you lacks whatever distinction is
thought to accrue from riches, so that rather you both have the
means in plentiful abundance for setting examples of good
deeds, particularly deeds of generosity. Both of you had fathers[3]

1. Beatus Rhenanus (Beat Bild, 1485–1547), the close friend of
Erasmus, was employed as an editor at the press of John Froben in
Basel. It was under his supervision that More's *Epigrams* were first
published, together with the *Utopia* and the *Epigrams* of Erasmus, in
March 1518. Another edition followed in November of the same year.
For the printing history of these volumes, see *CW 4,* clxxvii–cxciii.

2. Pirckheimer (1470–1530) served as councillor of Nuremberg
until 1522. As an advisor of the Emperor Maximilian, he was often
consulted on literary matters. Left a widower in 1504, he educated his
five daughters carefully with the result that they became as famous for
their learning as More's children.

3. More's father Sir John More (1453?–1530) became a sergeant-
at-law in 1503 and judge of the king's bench in 1523.

noted no less for their learning than for their distinguished birth. And so, since likeness and equality are the source of friendship, I have decided that it is very appropriate to call this work of More's to your attention so that, although for many other reasons you already honor the author with your affection, you may as a result of these *Epigrams* embrace, love, and esteem him even more. And furthermore, there is no one to whom these most delightful diversions can be sent more fittingly than to one who has himself frequently from time to time descended, as they say, into the same arena. That is to say, if anyone has himself at one time or another tried out his ingenuity at this kind of composition, he is the very man who will know how rare a thing is a learned epigram. Truly an epigram, as you know, must have wit combined with brevity; it must be lighthearted, and then it must end promptly with a witty point which the Greeks call ἐπιφώνημα. Surely one may find all these properties in these *Epigrams* of More's, especially in those which he himself composed; in the others, which are translated from the Greek, the credit for originality belongs to the ancients. Still, here, too, More deserves to be rated as high for translating well from a foreign tongue as for his own work. Undoubtedly the labor of a translator is often greater. This is so because the author is unfettered and freely at liberty to use whatever occurs to him, but the translator is required to keep something else continually in sight; that is, of course, what he has chosen to translate. Whenever this is the case, his skill is much more severely taxed than when he produces something of his own.

In both these fields Thomas More is very remarkable, for he composes most tastefully and translates most happily. How pleasantly his poetry flows! How utterly unforced is his work! How adroit it all is! Here is nothing harsh, nothing rough, nothing obscure. He is bright, sharp, a master of Latin. Furthermore, he seasons all his work with a certain very delightful humor so that I have never seen anything more charming. I could believe that the Muses conferred upon him all there is anywhere of mirth, charm, and wit. How gracefully he pokes fun at Sabinus[4] for bringing up another's children as his own. How wittily he ridicules Lalus, who went to such lengths in his desire to seem French. And yet his witticisms are by no means ill-natured, but rather are honest, sugar-coated, mild, anything but bitter. He provokes laughter, but in every case without pain; he ridicules, but without abuse. Just as Syrus in the play by Terence neatly praises Demea by saying "You are every inch pure wisdom," so it will be proper to say of More "He is every inch pure jest."[5]

At present Italy admires Pontanus and Marullus[6] more than most epigrammatists, but I would wager my life that there is just as much inherent skill in this author of ours and more profit, unless it is possible that someone think it very profitable when Marullus celebrates his Neaera and in many places speaks in riddles, acting like another Heraclitus,[7] or when Johannes Pontanus revives for us the lewdness of the ancient epigrammatists; and nothing could be more uninteresting or less worth reading for a man of principles, not to mention a man of Christian principles. Of course, it was their very great desire to imitate antiquity. To preserve the appearance of antiquity untainted, they avoided what was Christian just as Pomponius Laetus,[8] a man

4. For the poems on Sabinus, see *BL,* nos. 180, 189, and 204.

5. This sentence was deliberately omitted from the 1520 edition of the *Epigrams;* perhaps More felt that its humor was a bit undignified for an author who had become a member of the royal council in 1517. For the quotation from Terence, see *Adelphi,* III, iii, 40.

6. Giovanni Pontano (1426–1503) and Michael Marullus (d. 1500) were the best-known Neo-Latin poets in Italy.

7. Heraclitus of Ephesus (fl. 500 B.C.) whose cryptic sayings won for him the title "the obscure one."

8. Laetus (1428–98), the leader of the Roman Academy in the late fifteenth century, had a great reputation as a teacher. Among his pupils was More's friend, William Lily.

excessively Roman, avoided what was Greek, lest he destroy the purity of the Latin language. . . .[9]

I have only this left to say: when you have the opportunity, amid the duties which keep you so very busy conferring with embassies and administering the state, pick up this book, read it, and become an admirer of More, whose face, I think you have not yet seen; but you have known him a long time from his writings. Farewell, most illustrious sir.

Basel
February 23, 1518

On the Coronation Day of Henry VIII
Most Glorious and Blessed King
of the British Isles, and of Cath-
erine His Most Happy Queen[1]

A Poetical Expression of
Good Wishes by Thomas
More of London

If ever there was a day, England, if ever there was a time for you to give thanks to those above, this is that happy day, one to be marked with a pure white stone[2] and put in your calendar. This day is the limit of our slavery, the beginning of our freedom, the end of sadness, the source of joy, for this day consecrates a young man who is the everlasting glory of our time and makes him your king—the only king who is worthy to rule not merely a single people but the whole world—such a king as will

---

9. In his next two paragraphs (omitted here) Rhenanus discusses More's *Utopia* and praises William Lily, who had contributed translations to the Progymnasmata section of the *Epigrams*. For text and translation, see *BL,* pp. 5 and 127–28.

1. *BL,* No. 1. This is the first (and longest) of a group of five poems which More presented to Henry VIII at his coronation on June 24, 1509. Henry and Catherine of Aragon were married on June 11, 1509.

2. Lucky days were marked in the classical calendar with a white stone, unlucky days with a black one.

wipe the tears from every eye and put joy in the place of our long distress. Every heart smiles to see its cares dispelled, as the sun shines through scattered clouds. Now the people, freed, run before their king with bright faces. Their joy is almost beyond their own comprehension. They rejoice, they exult, they leap for joy and celebrate their having such a king. "The King" is all that any mouth can say.

The nobility, long since at the mercy of the dregs of the population, the nobility, whose title has been too long without meaning, now lifts its head, now rejoices in such a king, and has proper reason for rejoicing. The merchant, heretofore deterred by numerous taxes, now once again plows seas grown unfamiliar. Laws, heretofore powerless—yes, even laws put to unjust ends —now happily have regained their proper authority. All are equally happy. All weigh their earlier losses against the advantages to come. Now each man happily does not hesitate to show the possessions which in the past his fear kept hidden in dark seclusion. Now there is enjoyment in any profit which managed to escape the many very sly clutching hands of the many thieves. No longer is it a criminal offense to own property which was honestly acquired (formerly it was a serious offense). No longer does fear whisper, whisper secrets in one's ear, for no one has secrets either to keep or secretly to tell. Now it is a delight to ignore informers. Only ex-informers fear informers now.[3]

The people gather together, every age, both sexes, and all ranks. There is no reason why they should lurk in their homes and not take part while the king, after completion of the proper ceremonies, undertakes, amid happy auspices, the rule of Britain. Wherever he goes, the dense crowd in their desire to look upon him leaves hardly a narrow lane for his passage. The houses are filled to overflowing, the rooftops strain to support the weight of spectators. On all sides there arises a shout of new

3. In this paragraph and again later in the poem, More criticizes the policies of Henry VII's reign. The start of the new reign was marked by the execution of William Empson and Edmund Dudley, the principal agents of Henry VIII's father.

good will. Nor are the people satisfied to see the king just once; they change their vantage points time and time again in the hope that, from one place or another, they may see him again. Three times they delight to see him—and why not? This king who is as amiable as any creature in the realm of nature.

Among a thousand noble companions he stands out taller than any. And he has strength worthy of his regal person. His hand, too, is as skilled as his heart is brave, whether there is an issue to be settled by the naked sword, or an eager charge with leveled spears, or an arrow aimed to strike a target. There is fiery power in his eyes, beauty in his face, and such color in his cheeks as is typical of roses. In fact, that face, admirable for its animated strength, could belong to either a young girl or a man. Thus Achilles looked when he pretended to be a maiden, thus he looked when he dragged Hector behind his Thessalian steeds.[4]

If only nature would permit that, like his body, the outstanding excellence of his mind be visible. But, even so, his moral perfection does shine forth from his very countenance. His frank face reveals his noble heart. How ripe the wisdom in his judicious mind, how profound the calm of his untroubled breast! With what restraint he would endure his lot and be master of his fortune, good or bad! How great his care to honor modesty! How serene the mercy which warms his gentle heart! How far removed from arrogance his mind! Yes, of all these gifts, the very countenance of our prince, extraordinary as it is, wears upon itself sure evidence which cannot be falsified. On the other hand, how just he is, how skilled in ruling, how great the feeling of responsibility with which he treats his people— all this is made very plain by the expressions on our faces. These are our notable advantages. In that we are so happy and are winning freedom, in that fear, harm, danger, grief have vanished

4. Statius' *Achilleid* tells the story of Achilles' being hidden among the women of Scyros by Thetis his mother, who feared that he would die in the Trojan War. For Hector's death at the hands of Achilles, see Homer, *Iliad*, xxii.

and meanwhile peace, ease, joy, and laughter have returned—therein is revealed the excellence of our distinguished prince.

Unlimited power has a tendency to weaken good minds, and that even in the case of very gifted men. But howsoever dutiful he was before, his crown has brought our prince a character which deserves to rule, for he has provided promptly on his first day such advantages as few rulers have granted in extreme old age. He was quick to try and to imprison. If anyone by plots had harmed the realm or was an informer, he is closely fettered and confined, so that he himself suffers the woes which he imposed on many. Our prince opened the sea for trade. If any overharsh duties were required of the merchants, he lightened their load. And the long-scorned nobility recovered on our prince's first day the ancient rights of nobles. He now gives to good men the honors and public offices which used to be sold to evil men. By a happy reversal of circumstances, learned men now have the prerogatives which ignoramuses carried off in the past. Our prince without delay has restored to the laws their ancient force and dignity (for the end of law is the end of order). And although formerly each rank in the state was changing character completely, now at once every rank is restored. What if, in the hope of being kind to his people, he did seek in this connection to retract certain privileges which he knew his father had approved? In this he placed, as he should, his country before his father. This preference does not surprise me; what could lie beyond the powers of a prince whose natural gifts have been enhanced by a liberal education, a prince bathed by the nine sisters in the Castalian font and steeped in philosophy's own precepts? The whole people used to be, on many counts, in debt to the king; this in particular they feared. A king, since he could thus inspire fear, could also, if he wished, accumulate untold wealth. Our prince let them all off, freed them all from care, and entirely removed the evil practice which caused their anxious fears.

And so it is that subjects have always feared kings; but this king, who has banished fear, his subjects love.

O Prince, terror to your proud enemies but not to your own people, it is your enemies who fear you; we revere and love you. Our love for you will prove the reason for their fear. And thus it is that, in the absence of sycophants, your subjects' love and your enemies' fear will hedge you round in peace and safety. As for wars beyond the borders—if the French, for instance, join with the Scots[5]—no one is afraid, provided that England is not divided. And internal strife there will not be, for what cause, what reason, is there to provoke it? Most important, concerning your right and title to the crown, there is no opposition, nor can there be. You, all by yourself, represent both sides of the quarrel which usually arises;[6] the fact that both your parents were high-born disposes of this problem. And anyway the anger of the people, a wicked thing, common source of civil disturbance, is even more remote from you. To all your subjects you are as dear as your subjects to themselves. But just suppose that anger sent powerful leaders to war. Your nod will instantly put an end to the combat; so great a love, quite properly the product of your virtues, does your Sacred Majesty inspire. And whatever virtues your ancestors had, these are yours too, not excelled in ages past. For you, Sire, have your father's wisdom, you have your mother's kindly strength, the scrupulous intelligence of your paternal grandmother,[7] the noble heart of your mother's father.[8] What wonder, then, if England rejoices in a fashion heretofore unknown, since she has such a king as she never had before?

And then there is the fact that this joy, apparently as great as it could be, was increased by your marriage—a marriage which the kindly powers above arranged and in which they planned

5. Such an alliance was to occur in 1513 when, while Henry VIII invaded France, the Scots attacked on England's northern border.

6. Henry VIII, as the son of Elizabeth of York and Henry Tudor, united the houses of York and Lancaster in his own person. Dynastic conflict between the two houses had characterized the Wars of the Roses in the fifteenth century.

7. Margaret Beaufort (1443–1509), the mother of Henry VII.

8. Edward IV (1442–83).

well for you and yours. It was she, your wife, whom your people
were happy to see sharing your power. It was she for whom the
powers above care so much that they distinguish her and honor
her by marriage with you. She it is who could vanquish the ancient Sabine[9] women in devotion, and in dignity the holy, half-
divine heroines of Greece. She could equal the unselfish love
of Alcestis[1] or, in her unfailing judgment, outdo Tanaquil.[2] In
her expression, in her countenance, there is a remarkable beauty
uniquely appropriate for one so great and good. Cornelia,[3] that
famous mother, would yield to her in eloquence; Penelope,[4] in
loyalty to a husband. This lady, Sire, for love of you remained,
through many years and despite prolonged opposition, alone
and devoted.[5] Neither her own sister nor her native land could
win her from her way; neither her mother nor her father could
dissuade her. It was you, none other, whom she preferred to her
mother, sister, native land, and beloved father. This blessed lady
has joined to you in lasting alliance nations which are, in various
places, powerful. She is descended from great kings, to be sure;
and she will be the mother of kings as great as her ancestors. To
this time one anchor has protected your ship of state—a strong
one, yet only one. But your fruitful queen will present you with
a male heir, a protection in unbroken line, who shall be sup-

9. The mythical story of the rape of the Sabine women by the
followers of Romulus is told by Livy, I, 9.

1. The heroine of Euripides' tragedy who dies so that her husband
Admetus may be granted a longer life.

2. The legendary wife of Tarquinius Priscus (616–579 B.C.); she is
said, after the murder of her husband, to have secured the succession
of Servius Tullius.

3. The mother of the Gracchi (Tiberius and Gaius Sempronius)
and the daughter of Scipio Africanus; famous for her virtue and
learning.

4. The loyal wife of Odysseus.

5. Catherine had remained in England as a widow after the death
of Prince Arthur, Henry VIII's brother, in 1502. She resided, practi-
cally a prisoner, at Durham House in the Strand. The sister referred to
in the next sentence was Joanna, Queen of Castile, the mother of the
Emperor Charles V.

ported on every side. Great advantage is yours because of her, and similarly is hers because of you. There has been no other woman, surely, worthy to have you as husband, nor any other man worthy to have her as wife.

England, I hope you will bring incense and an offering even more effective, good hearts and innocent hands, in the hope that Heaven, as it has brought about this marriage, will also foster it, that the gift of power will be wielded with divine aid, and that, when these crowns have been long worn by our present king and queen, their grandson and their great-grandson will still be king.

On Suspicion, from the Greek[6]

The impression one creates has great influence, great weight, in the affairs of men. You have no desire to do any harm; but, if you seem to have, you are done for. Thus in Crotona they killed Philolaus[7] long ago in the mistaken belief that he wanted to play the tyrant.

Comments of a Rabbit Which, after
Eluding a Weasel, Fell into Nets
Spread by Hunters[8]

The weasel I did escape by darting through an opening off to one side, but—alas for me, miserable creature—then I rushed into the hunting nets of men. Now I cannot save my life or win quick death. They are saving me, alas, only to throw me to the ravening hounds. Now, while the hounds tear my body to pieces with their wicked teeth, a man looks on and smiles at the bloodshed. Insensate breed, more savage than any beast, to find cruel amusement in bitter slaughter!

6. *BL*, no. 7. Translated from the Greek Anthology (*AP*, vii, 126).

7. A Pythagorean philosopher, the disciple of Archytas.

8. Reminiscent of several poems in the Greek Anthology (cf. *AP*, ix, 14, 17, 18, 94, 371).

On a Comical Trial
from the Greek[9]

A case was being tried. The defendant was deaf, the plaintiff was deaf, and the judge himself was deafer than either. The plaintiff demanded five months' rent for the use of a house. The defendant replied, "I worked my mill all that night." The judge looked up at them and said, "What is your quarrel? She is the mother of both of you, is she not? Join in her support."

On a Certain Mean and
Very Stingy Bishop[1]

If I were to live as long as the Sibyl, I should never forget the kindness of the bishop. He is proprietor of many acres of rented land, possesses large cities, and travels with a retinue of a hundred attendants. And yet, when recently I approached him, although I am a man of very small property, still he received me and addressed me in really agreeable fashion. As a matter of fact, in order that I might taste a cup of his port before leaving, he himself extracted his key from his own purse.

Death Unassisted Kills Tyrants[2]

You who suffer cruelly at the hands of unjust men, no matter who you are, take hope. Let kindly hope alleviate your sufferings. A turn of fortune will improve your state—like the sun shining through scattered clouds—or the defender of liberty, Death, touched by pity, will with violent hand, while the tyrant rages, bring him down. Death will snatch even him away (the more to please you) and will lay him right before your feet. He who was so carried away by his great wealth and his empty pride, he who once upon a time amid his thronging courtiers was so bold, O, he will not be fierce, will not wear an expression

9. *BL,* no. 34. Translated from the Greek Anthology (*AP,* xi, 251).
1. *BL,* no. 53.
2. *BL,* no. 62.

of pride. He will be an object of pity, cast down from his high place, abandoned, helpless, penniless. What gift has life ever given you to compare with this gift from Death? He who used to inspire fear now will inspire laughter.

A Poem Translated from
an English Song[3]

Break, sad heart, pitiably engulfed in deepest woe. Let this be the end of your punishment. Show your mistress your bloody wounds. It is she only who will shortly separate us. Alas, how long shall I in my misery thus weep and complain? Come, dreaded death, and release me from monstrous woes.

A Jesting Poem to a Faithless
Mistress, Translated from
An English Song[4]

May the gods preserve us! What dreams I had last night! The whole universe was upset and fell to ruin. The sun's light did not survive, nor the moon's; and the swollen deep overwhelmed the land. Even more remarkable—you hear?—a voice seemed to say, "Just look, your mistress has broken the promise she made."

---

3. *BL*, no. 63. The English song which More translated has not been identified.

4. *BL*, no. 64. The song which More translated is no. 12 in the Fayrfax MS. (British Museum Additional MS. 5456):

> Benedicite! What dremyd I this nyght?
> Methought the worlde was turnyd up so downe,
> The son, the moone, had lost ther force and light;
> The see also drownyd both towre and towne:
> Yett more mervell how that I harde the sownde
> Of onys voice sayying, 'Bere in thy mynd,
> Thi lady hath forgoten to be kynd.'

On an Englishman Who Af-
fected to Speak French[5]

My friend and companion, Lalus, was born in England and brought up on our island. Nevertheless, although a mighty sea, their languages, and their customs separate Englishmen and the inhabitants of France, Lalus still is scornful of all things English. All things French he admires and wants. He struts about in French dress; he is very fond of little French capes. He is happy with his belt, his purse, his sword—if they are French; with his hat, his beret, his cap—if they are French. He delights in French shoes, French underclothes, and, to put it briefly, in an outfit French from head to toe. Why, he even has one servant, and he is a Frenchman. But France herself, I think, could not, if she tried, treat him in more French a fashion: he pays the servant nothing, like a Frenchman; he clothes him in worn-out rags, in the French manner; he feeds him little and that little poor, as the French do; he works him hard, like the French; he strikes him often, like a Frenchman; at social gatherings, and on the street, and in the market-place, and in public he quarrels with him and abuses him always in the French fashion. What! Have I said that he does this in French fashion? I should say rather in half-French fashion. For, unless I am mistaken, he is as familiar with the French language in general as a parrot is with Latin. Still he swells with pride and is, naturally, pleased with himself if he gets off three words in French. If there is anything he cannot say in French, then he tries to say it—granted the words are not French—at least with a French accent, with open palate, a shrill sort of sound, effeminate, like women's chatter, but lisping prettily you may be sure, as though his mouth were full of beans, and pronouncing with emphasis the letters which the foolish French avoid as the cock avoids the fox or the sailor the cliffs. And so it is with this kind of French accent that he speaks Latin, English, Italian,

5. *BL,* no. 77. This epigram was written about 1513.

Spanish, German, and every language except only French; for French is the one language he speaks with an English accent. But if any native of Britain in this haughty way scorns his native land in an apelike effort to feign and counterfeit the follies of the French, I think that such a man has been made mad by drinking of the River Gallus. Therefore, since he is trying to change from Englishman to Frenchman, order him, ye gods, to change from cock to capon.[6]

The Difference between a Tyrant and a King[7]

A king who respects the law differs from dread tyrants thus: a tyrant thinks of his subjects as slaves; a king, as his own children.

That the Tyrant's Life Is Troubled[8]

Great anxiety wears away the waking hours of the mighty tyrant; peace comes at night if it comes at all. But the tyrant does not rest more comfortably on any soft bed than the poor man does on the hard ground. And so, tyrant, in view of this fact, the happiest part of your life is that in which you willingly become no better than a beggar.

That the Good King Is a Father Not a Master, Iambics[9]

The king who performs his duty properly will never lack children; he is father to the whole kingdom. And so it is that a true king is abundantly blessed in having as many children as he has subjects.

6. More puns on the various meanings of the word "Gallus": (1) a Frenchman, (2) a river of Phrygia, (3) a eunuch priest of the goddess Cybele, and (4) a cock.

7. *BL,* no. 91.　　8. *BL,* no. 92.　　9. *BL,* no. 93.

On the Good King and His People[1]

A kingdom in all its parts is like a man; it is held together by
natural affection. The king is the head; the people form the
other parts. Every citizen the king has he considers a part of
his own body (that is why he grieves at the loss of a single one).
His subjects exert themselves in the king's behalf, and they all
look upon him as the head for which they provide the body.

That the Tyrant While He Sleeps
Is No Different from
the Commoner[2]

Well then, you madman, it is pride which makes you carry
your head so high—because the throng bows to you on bended
knee, because the people rise and uncover for you, because you
have in your power the life and death of many. But whenever
sleep secures your body in inactivity, then, tell me, where is this
glory of yours? Then you lie, useless creature, like a lifeless log
or like a recent corpse. Under these conditions, if you were not
lying protected, like a coward, unseen indoors, your own life
would be at the disposal of any man.

On Kings, Good and Bad[3]

What is a good king? He is a watchdog, guardian of the flock.
By his barking he keeps the wolves from the sheep. What is the
bad king? He is the wolf.

On a Rapist and His Lawyer[4]

A girl charged that she had been raped. There was no deny-
ing the accusation. The rapist was doomed. But his clever
lawyer unexpectedly parted the defendant's clothing and extracted the essential cause of the complaint. Said the lawyer,

1. *BL,* no. 94.   2. *BL,* no. 96.   3. *BL,* no. 97.
4. *BL,* no. 98.

"My girl, is this the part which was in that space?" The girl was so ashamed that she replied, "No, not that." The jubilant lawyer said, "Your honor, we have won this case. This is the girl who ought to know. She herself says, 'Not that.' Just look; if 'not that' is true, then she admits that she was not raped."

On the Futility of This Life[5]

We are all shut up in the prison of this world under sentence of death. In this prison none escapes death. The land within the prison is divided into many sections, and men build their dwellings in different sections. As if the prison were a kingdom, the inmates struggle for position. The avaricious man hoards up wealth within the obscure prison. One—within the limits of his prison—wanders freely about, another lies shackled in his cave; there are slaves and kings, men who sing and men who groan. And still, from this prison which we love as no prison should be loved, we are released only by death in one form or another.

A King Is Protected, Not by a Corps of Guards, but by His Own Good Qualities[6]

Not fear (accompanied as it is by hatred), not towering palaces, not wealth wrung from a plundered people protects a king. The stern bodyguard, hired for a pittance, offers no protection, for the guard will serve a new master as he served the old. He will be safe who so rules his subjects that they judge none other more suitable to their interests.

The Consent of the People Both Bestows and Withdraws Sovereignty[7]

Any one man who has command of many men owes his authority to those whom he commands; he ought to have com-

5. *BL,* no. 101.   6. *BL,* no. 102.   7. *BL,* no. 103.

mand not one instant longer than his subjects wish. Since kings, not their own masters, rule on sufferance, why are they proud?

On Fame and Popular Opinion[8]

Most men congratulate themselves if they attain to fame, empty though it is; and, because they are light-minded, they are lifted to the stars by the fickle wind of opinion. Why do you derive satisfaction from the comments of the populace? In their blindness they often interpret what is best as a failing and thoughtlessly approve what is very reprehensible. You hang everlastingly upon a stranger's opinion for fear that some cobbler will retract the praise he has conferred. Perhaps the man whose praise makes you proud is mocking you. Though he praise you from his heart, that praise is ephemeral. What does fame do for you? Though you be praised by all the world, still if you have an aching joint, what does fame do for you?

To Candidus: How to Choose a Wife, a Poem in Iambic Dimeter Brachycatalectic[9]

Your time of life, Candidus, is now reaching a point where it suggests that at last you reject temporary attachments, that you cease at last to pursue haphazard love affairs, and that you find a girl to take as wife formally and in mutual devotion. Let her be fruitful and add charming children to your most splendid line. Your father did as much for you. Hand on with increase to your descendants what you have already received from your ancestors.

Still, let not your primary concern be how much dowry she brings or how beautiful she is. Weakness marks any love which arises either from a blind impulse roused by mere beauty or from a base love of money.

8. *BL,* no. 114.
9. *BL,* no. 125. Perhaps the most popular of all More's *Epigrams.* For a modern comment, with French translation, see *Moreana, 26* (1970), 18–32.

The man who loves for money's sake loves only money. As soon as he acquires the money, his fleeting love is gone and dies almost before it is born. And the money, which in his miserable selfishness he had coveted earlier, cannot help him in the least later on when he is required, howsoever unwilling, to keep the wife he does not love.

What is beauty? Does it not fail in sickness, perish with time like a flower in the sun? Then, when the bloom leaves her cheek, a love secured only by such ties as these breaks free and is gone forever. Only a man of intelligence and foresight, with reason for his guide, can enter upon true love. True love is inspired, with happy promise, by respect for a woman's chastity, a noble gift which endures, does not fail in sickness, does not perish with the years.

And so, my friend, if you desire to marry, first observe what kind of parents the lady has, in the hope that, as a mother, she may be endowed with the best of characters for her tender infant to acquire—along with mother's milk—and to imitate.

Next see to this: what sort of personality she has; how agreeable she is. Let her expression be calm and without severity. And, too, let her modesty bring blushes to her cheeks; let her glance be not provocative. Let her be mild-mannered, not inclined to bold embraces. Let her glances be restrained; let her have no roving eye. In her speech let there be never a trace of pointless garrulity or of boorish taciturnity. Let her be either educated or capable of being educated. Happy is the woman whose education permits her to derive from the best of ancient works the principles which confer a blessing on life. Armed with this learning, she would not yield to pride in prosperity, nor to grief in distress—even though misfortune strike her down. For this reason your lifetime companion will be ever agreeable, never a trouble or a burden. If she is well instructed herself, then some day she will teach your little grandsons, at an early age, to read.

You will find it a pleasure to leave the company of men and, after your accomplished wife has embraced you, to lie at ease while she encourages you, while under her dexterous touch the stringed music swells, while in a sweet voice (as sweet, Procne, as your sister's)[1] she sings pleasant songs such as Apollo would be glad to hear. Then it will be your pleasure to spend days and nights in pleasant and intelligent conversation, listening to the sweet words which most charmingly flow from her ever honeyed mouth. By her comments she would restrain you if ever vain success should exalt you or speechless grief should cast you down. When she speaks, it will be difficult to judge between her extraordinary ability to say what she thinks and her thoughtful understanding of all kinds of affairs.

I should think that the wife of the bard Orpheus[2] long ago was such a woman; he would never have taken the trouble to recover from the dead, by impious effort, an uncultivated wife.

Such a woman, I believe, was Ovid's famous daughter,[3] who could rival in poetical composition even her own father.

Such a woman, I suspect, was Tullia,[4] most beloved daughter of a most learned father.

Such a woman was the mother of the two Gracchi.[5] She taught her sons right principles; she accomplished no less as their teacher than she did as their mother.

Why do I continue to contemplate ancient times? After all, our age, rude though it is, possesses one maiden—but only one —so extraordinary that our own age would prefer her to most and compare her with any of those famous women of so long ago. Borne high upon the soaring wings of fame, she is now heeded even in the remotest parts of Britain, an incomparable girl, a Cassandra,[6] the admiration and glory of the whole world, not merely of her own country.

1. Philomela, who was, in Greek fable, changed into a nightingale after her rape by Tereus, King of Thrace.

2. Eurydice, whom Orpheus sought to recover from Hades.

3. The gifted Perilla of *Tristia*, III, 7, was probably Ovid's stepdaughter.

4. The daughter of Marcus Tullius Cicero.

5. Tanaquil. See above, p. 135, n. 2.

6. The girl to whom More refers has not been identified with certainty. Henry VIII's sisters Margaret and Mary have been suggested as candidates, and Catherine of Aragon might be added to the list. Cassandra, the daughter of Priam, was the doomed prophetess of Troy.

And so speak up, Candidus. Suppose you, too, had for wife a girl such as those I mentioned above—then, although you might perceive in her some lack of beauty, although you might complain because you are too little enriched by her dowry, still here is the truth of the matter: "Whoever she is, if a woman is agreeable, she is goodlooking enough; and no man possesses more than he who is content with what he has."

May my own wife cease to love me if I am not telling you the truth, my friend. If nature has denied the gift of beauty to a girl, yes, though she be blacker than coal, still, if she has this inborn gift of virtue, she would be in my eyes fairer than the swan. If elusive fortune has denied her a dowry, yes, though she be poorer than Irus,[7] still, if she has this inborn gift of virtue, she would be in my eyes richer, Croesus,[8] than you.

Epitaphivm Abyngdonii Cantoris[9]

Attrahat huc oculos, aures attraxerat olim
　　Nobilis Henricus cantor Abyngdonius.
Vnus erat nuper mira qui uoce sonaret.
　　Organa qui scite tangeret unus erat.
Vellensis primo templi decus, inde sacellum
　　Rex illo uoluit nobilitare suum.
Nunc illum regi rapuit deus, intulit astris,
　　Ipsis ut noua sit gloria caelitibus.

Epitaph of Abyngdon, the Singer

Let the famed singer, Henry Abyngdon, draw your eyes to this, his tomb; there was a time when his appeal was to the ear. Not long ago he sang in a voice marvelous beyond compare and

---

7. A beggar in the household of Odysseus.

8. The fabulously wealthy King of Lydia (560–546 B.C.).

9. *BL,* no. 141. More's Latin is given for this poem and the following two (*BL,* nos. 142 and 143); the point of the verses depends upon the metrical form in which they were written. Henry Abyngdon (c. 1418–c. 1497), a singer, organist, and composer, was first master of

played the organ with incomparable skill. At first he was the pride of the church at Wells; then the king wanted him to lend his fame to the Chapel Royal. Now God has taken him away from the king and installed him among the stars to add glory to the very inhabitants of heaven.

Altervm de Eodem[1]

Hic iacet Henricus, semper pietatis amicus.
Nomen Abyngdon erat, si quis sua nomina quaerat.
Vuellis hic ecclesia fuerat succentor in alma,
Regis et in bella cantor fuit ipse capella.
Millibus in mille cantor fuit optimus ille.
Praeter et haec ista, fuit optimus orgaquenista.
Nunc igitur, Christe, quoniam tibi seruijt iste
    Semper in orbe soli, da sibi regna poli.

Another Epitaph on the Same Man

Here lies Henry, the constant friend of piety. Abyngdon was his family name, if anyone should want that too. He was once subchanter of the church at Wells, which cherished him; and later he became chanter in the beautiful Chapel Royal. He was the best singer among a million. And besides this he was the best of organists. And so now, Christ, since he served You always on earth, admit him to the Kingdom of Heaven.

In Ianvm Haeredem Abyngdonii

Scripsi elegum carmen, Iano me haerede rogante,
    Quod tumulum Henrici signet Abyngdonij.
Displicet, et doctis bene displicuisset, at illi

---

the children of the Chapel Royal. Janus, Henry's heir, has not been identified. For a full discussion of the three poems, see Susan L. Holahan, "More's Epigrams on Henry Abyngdon," *Moreana, 17* (1968), 21–26.

1. This poem is in rhymed medieval verse.

Displicet hoc tantum, si quid inest melius.
Non resonant isti uersus, ait. Illico sensi
    Qualeis lactucas talia labra petant.
Ridendos ergo ridens effutio uersus.
    Hos uorat applaudens Ianus utraque manu.
Hos tumulo inscalpsit, sub eundem protinus obdi
    Atque ijsdem dignus uersibus ipse legi.
Ante retroque bifrons Ianus deus omnia uidit.
    Talpa effrons uidet hic Ianus utrinque nihil.

On Janus, Abyngdon's Heir

I wrote a poem in elegiac couplets to mark the tomb of Henry Abyngdon at the request of his heir, Janus. Janus did not like it—and it might well have failed to please learned men. But Janus disliked only its better parts. "These verses of yours do not rhyme," he said. I realized at once what kind of inferior food such lips as his like. So for a joke I blurted out some ridiculous verses. These Janus received with enthusiasm and applause. These are the verses he had inscribed on the tomb. He deserves to be thrust forthwith into the same tomb and to be distinguished by the same epitaph. The two-faced god, Janus, saw everything in front and behind him. This Janus, like a sightless mole, sees nothing before or behind.

To a Courtier[2]

You often boast to me that you often make frivolous comments for the king's ear without restraint and in accordance with your own inclination. This is like playing with tamed lions —often it is harmless, but every time there is the danger of harm. Often in anger he roars for no known reason, and sud-

---

2. *BL,* no. 144. Cf. More's advice to Thomas Cromwell: a counsellor should tell the king "what he ought to do but never what he is able to do.... For if a lion knew his own strength, hard were it for any man to rule him" (Roper, *Life of More,* in *Two Early Tudor Lives,* ed. R. S. Sylvester and D. P. Harding [New Haven, 1962], p. 228).

denly what was just now a game brings death. Your pleasure
in this matter is not safe enough to relieve you of anxiety. It is
a great pleasure. As for me, let my pleasure be less great—
and safe.

On a Girl Who Feigned Rape[3]

When a certain wicked young man saw a girl all by herself
and thought that this was his chance, he put his eager arms
around her—although she was reluctant—and tried to kiss her
and was ready to give her more than kisses. She struggled
against him and angrily cited the law which exacts capital punishment of one who is guilty of rape. But still, with a young
man's eagerness, the shameless fellow did his best to take her
either by coaxing or by threatening. She resisted both coaxing
and threats; she screamed. She kicked him, bit him, struck him.
There came upon him an anger which was at least as great as
his lust. Savagely he said, "You fool, are you going to keep this
up? I swear to you by this sword"—and he drew it—"if you do
not lie down, get ready, and keep quiet, I am going to leave
you." Terrified by so dire a threat she lay down at once and
said, "Go ahead, but it is an act of violence."

On an Astrologer[4]

While astrologers (kept busy by our mistaking them for
prophets) are naming your destiny in accordance with the
position of the stars, while this star is promising and that one
threatening, your mind swings back and forth between hope
and fear. If good fortune is to come, it will come, though the
stars keep silent; and unexpected good luck usually gives more
pleasure. If, on the other hand, bad luck is to come, then it will
be advantageous for you to remain in ignorance of it for a
while and to make pleasant use of the time until it arrives. In
fact, these are my instructions: "Even though the very fates

3. *BL,* no. 149.   4. *BL,* no. 151.

forbid, see that your mind is untroubled and spends its time merrily."

On Some Sailors Who Made Their
Confessions to a Monk dur-
ing a Storm and Then
Threw Him Overboard[5]

When the heaving sea in a roaring storm was rising high and when the anger of the waves was raging against the struggling ship, uneasy conscience descended upon the frightened sailors. They cried, "Our ill-spent lives have brought on these ills." There was a monk among the passengers. Into his ear they hastily unloaded their sins. But when they observed that the sea had not in the least calmed down, that, rather, the ship was just barely afloat on the ravening waters, one of them cried out, "No wonder our ship is barely afloat! All this time it has been weighed down by our cargo of sin. Why not throw overboard this monk who now carries the guilt of all of us, and let him take our sins away with him?" The sailors approve the suggestion; they lay hold of the fellow; they heave him into the sea. And—so they say—the ship sailed lighter than before. From this story—yes, this story—learn how heavy is a load of sin, since a ship cannot sustain its weight.

To Candidus, a Pastor Who
Led an Evil Life[6]

My dear Candidus, you have been made pastor of a large congregation. Therefore, I heartily congratulate you and your flock. Either partiality has damaged my judgment, or it is not possible that your flock ever before had such a priest. You do

5. *BL,* no. 157. For a similar situation, see Erasmus' colloquy, "The Shipwreck" in *The Colloquies of Erasmus,* tr. Craig R. Thompson (Chicago, 1965), pp. 138–46.

6. *BL,* no. 158.

not have worldly understanding to make you proud; in fact, such understanding is of no use to your congregation. Moreover, yours are rare virtues; similarly rare, I believe, were men like you among the priests of old. Your life can function as a conspicuous model by which your people can decide what to do and what to avoid. It remains only to advise them that they observe you closely, avoid what you do, and do what you avoid.

Fable of the Sick Fox
and the Lion[7]

While a fox lay sick in a narrow cave, a lion endowed with persuasive speech took his place at the entrance. Said he, "Tell me, my friend, you are not sick, are you? You will soon recover if you let me lick you. You just do not know the power of my tongue." "Your tongue," said the fox, "has healing powers; but the harm comes from the notorious fact that your admittedly good tongue has bad neighbors."

An Epitaph for James
King of the Scots[8]

It is I, James, King of the Scots, brave and ill-starred enemy of a friendly power, who am interred beneath this sod. Had my loyalty been equal to my courage, the sequel with its shame for me would not have happened. But, alas, I must not boast and I will not complain—therefore, I shall say no more. And I hope, O chattering Infamy, that you may be willing to keep silent. You kings (I was once a king myself) I warn not to let loyalty become, as it often does, a meaningless word.

7. *BL,* no. 162.
8. *BL,* no. 166. James IV of Scotland, who had married Henry VIII's sister Margaret in 1503, was killed at the Battle of Flodden Field in 1513.

On Brixius as Plagiarist[9]

No one cultivates the ancient poets more than you or more assiduously reaps their harvest, for there is not one among the ancient poets from whose works, here or there, you have not, with greedy hand, plucked blossoms and buds; and you immediately repay the poet by the great honor of being slipped in with what you write. And you do confer a favor upon the poet, for what you have gathered proclaims its origin and gleams in the midst of your verse more brightly than the stars in the night sky. You, friend of all poets, begrudge none of them this great honor, lest one of them, the glory of an age that is past, weep at your neglect. Therefore, lest the hallowed measures of the poets perish of long disuse, you endow with new luster authors whom time has unjustly claimed for her own. This is skilfully to renew what is old, as happy an occupation as any. O blessed poetical skill—and yet whoever, by the kind of skill you have, lends freshness to what is old, at the same time, where he has no skill (sweat though he may), imposes senescence on what is new.

What Is the Best Form
of Government[1]

You ask which governs better, a king or a senate. Neither, if (as is frequently the case) both are bad. But if both are good, then I think that the senate, because of its numbers, is the better and that the greater good lies in numerous good men. Perhaps it is difficult to find a group of good men; even more frequently

9. *BL,* no. 177. One of a sequence of poems against the French humanist Germain de Brie of Auxerre (Germanus Brixius, d. 1538), whose poem, *Chordigerae Navis Conflagratio* (1513), had been attacked by More. Brixius replied in his *Antimorus* of 1518. For a full account of the quarrel, see E. F. Rogers, ed., *The Correspondence of Sir Thomas More* (Princeton, 1947), p. 212.

1. *BL,* no. 182. The Latin title of this poem ("Quis Optimus Reipublicae Status") is echoed by that of More's *Utopia (De Optimo Reipublicae Statu,* etc.).

it is easy for a monarch to be bad. A senate would occupy a position between good and bad; but hardly ever will you have a king who is not either good or bad. An evil senator is influenced by advice from better men than he; but a king exercises the only influence on his advisers. A senator is elected by the people to rule; a king attains this end by being born. In the one case blind chance is supreme; in the other, a reasonable agreement. The one feels that he was made senator by the people; the other feels that the people were created for him so that, of course, he may have subjects to rule.

A king in his first year is always very mild indeed. In every year, therefore, the consul will be a new king. Over a long time a selfish king will wear his people out. If a consul is evil, there is hope of improvement. I am not swayed by the famous proverb which recommends that one endure the well-fed fly lest a hungry one take its place. It is a mistake to believe that a selfish king can be satisfied; such a leech never leaves flesh until it is drained.

But, you say, a serious disagreement impedes a senate's decisions, while no one disagrees with a king. But that is the worse evil of the two, for when there is a difference of opinion about important matters—but say, what started you on this inquiry anyway? Is there anywhere a people upon whom you yourself, by your own decision, can impose either a king or a senate? If this does lie within your power, you are king. Stop considering to whom you may give power. The prior question is whether to give it at all.

On the King and the Peasant[2]

A forest-bred peasant, more naïve than Faunus or a Satyr, came to town. See there! the inhabitants have taken places on either side to fill the avenue, and throughout the city all one could hear was the cry, "The king is coming." The peasant was

2. *BL,* no. 185. This poem recalls the anecdote of the Anemolian Ambassadors in the *Utopia* (see *CW 4,* 153–57).

roused by the strange new cry and conceived a desire to see what the crowd was watching for so eagerly. Suddenly the king rode by, easily distinguished, clad in gold, escorted by a large company, and astride a tall horse. Then truly did the crowd roar: "Long live the king"; and with rapt expressions they gazed up at the king. The peasant called out, "Where is the king? Where is the king?" And one of the bystanders replied, "There he is, the one mounted high on that horse over there." The peasant said, "Is that the king? I think you are fooling me. He seems to me to be a man in an embroidered garment."

On the Anxious Life of Rulers[3]

Excessive power invariably brings miserable worries. Power, tormented by ever present fears, does not venture out unless surrounded by many armed men, does not eat food which has not been tasted in advance. Certainly these precautions are aids to safety; yet they show that a man is not safe if he cannot be safe without them. A bodyguard, for instance, shows the danger of violence, a taster shows the danger of poison. And so what place is without fear in a life where the very means of repelling future terrors themselves engender terrors right at hand?

To One Who Said That His Poems Would Not Lack Genius[4]

A witty epigram of the Spanish poet[5] contains this thought: "To live, a book must have genius." Ever since you read this verse, you have been getting ready—with all the intelligence you have, but that is no intelligence—to write poetry yourself. You care nothing for the theme or style of your song, such hope have you that whatever you sing will live by its genius. I point this out, you great genius, because you believe that later on, from some source or other, genius will attach itself to your Muse. But you ought rather to hope (this hope will be fulfilled)

3. *BL,* no. 222.   4. *BL,* no. 226.
5. Martial; More quotes *Epigrams,* VI, 60, 10.

that this book of yours may lack genius, since it also lacks character and since any genius which prolongs the book's life will be one of the thousand evil geniuses which attend you. But, even so, your book will not live—if you can take the word of the same prophet—for life is not merely to exist but rather to flourish. Still, if, for a book, to live is to wither under the shame of suppression, then may it be your privilege to live that death forever.

On the Lust for Power[6]

Among many kings there will be scarcely one, if there is really one, who is satisfied to have one kingdom. Among many kings there will be scarcely one, if there is really one, who rules a single kingdom well.

To Busleiden on His Splendid House at Mechlin[7]

While recently I gazed with fascinated eyes at the tasteful decorations in your house, Busleiden, I wondered by what incantation you had charmed the fates so as to bring back so many ancient masters. For I think that only the hands of Daedalus could have built that famous house of yours with its artfully devised passages. The pictures there Apelles seems to have painted. The sculptures one might believe to be the work of Myron. When I looked upon the terra-cottas I thought them the product of Lysippus' art. The statues made me think of the master Praxiteles. Couplets identify every work of art, and such couplets as Vergil would have been glad to write, if he did not actually write them. Only the organ which produces varied tones by modulation is, I think, beyond the powers even of the ancients. And so your whole house is either an accomplishment of

6. *BL,* no. 227.

7. *BL,* no. 236. Jerome de Busleiden (c. 1470–1517), a famous lawyer and humanist, was a member of the Great Council at Mechlin and Provost of Aire. His magnificent house is now the town museum.

antiquity or a recent accomplishment such as to surpass antiquity. Well, may this new house be slow, may it be late, in growing old. And may the house in its old age still see its master, not even then grown old.

To the Reader, on the Translation of the New Testament by
Erasmus of Rotterdam[8]

A holy work, an immortal accomplishment of the learned Erasmus is coming out; and how great are the advantages it brings to men! for the new law was first marred by the ancient translator and then further damaged by the inaccurate copying of scribes. Jerome long ago may have removed errors, but his readings, excellent as they were, have been lost by long neglect. That is why the whole work has been corrected and translated anew. And Christ's new law shines with new splendor. Erasmus has not ostentatiously disputed the text word by word; he has considered inviolable whatever is merely acceptable. And so it is that, if anyone skims over this version in rapid flight, he would perhaps think that nothing of importance is afoot, but, if he retraces the author's steps closely, he will decide that there is no greater or more helpful work.

Epitaph on the Tomb of Jane,[9] Deceased Wife of More, Who In-
tends the Same Tomb for His
Own Use and That of Al-
ice, His Second Wife

My beloved wife, Jane, lies here. I, Thomas More, intend that this same tomb shall be Alice's and mine, too. One of these

---

8. *BL,* no. 239. Erasmus' new translation was first published in 1516.
9. *BL,* no. 242. This is the last poem in the 1518 edition of the *Epigrams.* For the 1520 edition More added eleven new poems. Jane Colt, whom More had married in 1505, died in 1511. More's second wife was the widow Alice Middleton.

ladies, my wife in the days of my youth, has made me father of a son and three daughters; the other has been as devoted to her stepchildren (a rare attainment in a stepmother) as very few mothers are to their own children. The one lived out her life with me, and the other still lives with me on such terms that I cannot decide whether I did love the one or do love the other more. O, how happily we could have lived all three together if fate and morality permitted. Well, I pray that the grave, that heaven, will bring us together. Thus death will give what life could not.

On the Cat and the Mouse[1]

When I offered to the cat the mouse I had taken from a trap she did not immediately and ravenously eat her prize. With great restraint she placed her trembling prey on open ground and happily toyed with it in extraordinary fashion. She twitched her tail, watched the mouse with threatening gaze, and playfully turned her head from side to side. Gently, with a paw, she provoked the terrified mouse into moving, and when it started to move she stopped it; and alternately she let it go and caught it again. Soon with her paws she tossed it up high and caught it in her mouth. Then she walked away from it and gave it even now the hope of escaping when there was no escape. She lay down to watch at a distance, and, as the mouse made off, she joyfully leaped upon it and returned to the spot from which it had fled. Again she left it, and, with amazing understanding of the poor mouse's intentions, the wicked creature subjected it to this and that ordeal. While she was repeating this performance and confidently going farther away, the mouse suddenly found a crack and was gone. The cat rushed to the hole and sat on guard—in vain. The mouse, protected in its hiding place, was safe from its enemy. The trap would have caused the death of the mouse if the cat, usually fatal to mice, had not become its protector and its salvation.

1. *BL,* no. 246.

He Expresses His Joy at Finding
Safe and Sound Her Whom
He Had Loved as
a Mere Boy[2]

Are you really still alive, Elizabeth, dearer to me in my early
years than I was myself, and are you restored to my sight! What
evil chance has kept you from me all these many years! When I
was just a boy, I saw you first; now on the threshold of old age,
I see you again. Sixteen years I had lived—you were about two
years younger—when your face inspired me with innocent
devotion. That face is now no part of your appearance; where
has it gone? When the vision I once loved comes before me, I
see, alas, how utterly your actual appearance fails to resemble
it. The years, always envious of young beauty, have robbed you
of yourself but have not robbed me of you. That beauty of
countenance to which my eyes so often clung now occupies my
heart. It is natural for a dying fire, though buried in its own
cold ashes, to flare up upon application of the bellows. And
changed though you are, you have caused an old flame to gleam
again because of this recent reminder. There comes now to my
mind that distant day which first revealed you to me as you
played amid a group of girls; this was a time when your yellow
hair enhanced the pure white of your neck; your lips by con-
trast with your face were like roses in the snow; your eyes, like
stars, held my eyes fast and through them made their way into
my heart: I was helpless, as though stunned by a lightning-
stroke, when I gazed and continued to gaze upon your face.
Then, too, our comrades laughed at our love, so awkward, so
frank, and so obvious. Thus did your beauty take me captive.
Either yours was perfect beauty, or I lent it more perfection
than it had; perhaps the stirrings of adolescence and the ardor
which accompanies the approach of manhood were the reason,

2. *BL,* no. 247. The "Elizabeth" of More's poem (presumably
written in 1519 when he was forty-one) has not been identified.

or perhaps certain stars we shared at birth had influenced both
our hearts. In any case a companion and confidante of yours in
a talkative mood revealed that your heart, too, was moved.
On this account a chaperon was imposed upon us, and a door
strong enough to thwart our very destiny kept apart a pair
whom the stars would bring together. And then that notable
day after so many years brought us together, far separated
though we were in the pursuit of our different destinies. Oh
that kindly treasured day when we met—it brought to me more
than a lifetime of pleasure in the encounter which showed me
you were alive. Once upon a time you innocently stole my heart;
now too, and innocently still, you are dear to me. Our love was
blameless; if duty could not keep it so, that day itself would be
enough to keep love blameless still. Well, I beg the saints above,
who, after twenty-five years, have kindly brought us together in
good health, that I may be preserved to see you safe and sound
again at the end of twenty-five years more.

Thomas More Greets His Beloved Children, Margaret, Elizabeth, Cecilia, and John[3]

I hope that a letter to all of you may find my four children in
good health and that your father's good wishes may keep you
so. In the meantime, while I make a long journey, drenched by
a soaking rain, and while my mount, too frequently, is bogged
down in the mud, I compose these verses for you in the hope
that, although unpolished, they may give you pleasure. From
these verses you may gather an indication of your father's feel-
ings for you—how much more than his own eyes he loves you;
for the mud, the miserably stormy weather, and the necessity
for driving a diminutive horse through deep waters have not
been able to distract his thoughts from you or to prevent his
proving that, wherever he is, he thinks of you. For instance,

3. *BL,* no. 248.

when—and it is often—his horse stumbles and threatens to fall, your father is not interrupted in the composition of his verses. Poetry often springs from a heart which has no feeling; these verses a father's love provides—along with a father's natural anxiety. It is not so strange that I love you with my whole heart, for being a father is not a tie which can be ignored. Nature in her wisdom has attached the parent to the child and bound them spiritually together with a Herculean knot. This tie is the source of my consideration for your immature minds, a consideration which causes me to take you often into my arms. This tie is the reason why I regularly fed you cake and gave you ripe apples and fancy pears. This tie is the reason why I used to dress you in silken garments and why I never could endure to hear you cry. You know, for example, how often I kissed you, how seldom I whipped you. My whip was invariably a peacock's tail. Even this I wielded hesitantly and gently so that sorry welts might not disfigure your tender seats. Brutal and unworthy to be called father is he who does not himself weep at the tears of his child. How other fathers act I do not know, but you know well how gentle and devoted is my manner toward you, for I have always profoundly loved my own children and I have always been an indulgent parent—as every father ought to be. But at this moment my love has increased so much that it seems to me I used not to love you at all. This feeling of mine is produced by your adult manners, adult despite your tender years; by your instincts, trained in noble principles which must be learned; by your pleasant way of speaking, fashioned for clarity; and by your very careful weighing of every word. These characteristics of yours so strangely tug at my heart, so closely bind me to you, my children, that my being your father (the only reason for many a father's love) is hardly a reason at all for my love of you. Therefore, most dearly beloved children all, continue to endear yourselves to your father and, by those same acomplishments which make me think that I had not loved you before, make me think hereafter (for you can do it) that I do not love you now.

He Apologizes because in the Midst
of a Conversation with a Promi-
nent Cleric He Had Failed to Notice a Certain Noble Lady Who
Entered the Room and Stood
beside Them for Some Time
as They Talked[4]

Mighty prelate, on that recent occasion when Your Excel-
lency saw fit to pay me a call and to enter my humble house,
while you were conversing with me so pleasantly that I was entirely preoccupied with your words, observe! a lady entered—as
my servants informed me too late, yesterday in fact, when the
matter was many days past. The lady is remarkable for her noble
elegance; but her beauty surpasses her elegance as her goodness
surpasses her beauty. She came right up to our couch and stood
very near me, right at my elbow. She examined some choice
coins of ancient beauty and, famous herself, enjoyed the famous
portraits thereon. As she did me the favor of taking some sweet
from my scanty table, an even greater sweetness emanated from
her sweet face. And yet my eyes failed to observe even so brilliant
a beauty as hers. Alas, for the more than insensate stupidity
which was mine. Now I forgive my servants' not warning me.
Surely no one of them thought his master so dull. O eyes, which
used to be able to perceive from a distance such splendor radiat-
ing from any girl! Have I grown old? And is perception dulled
in this body of mine? Or did an evil spirit attend my rising that
morning? Or did you beguile me with your charming conversation so that I was unable to be aware of anything but you?
Orpheus, by his skill with the lyre, charmed wild beasts. I
similarly am charmed by your delightful words. But that presence of yours imposed a great risk that the lady feel she had
been neglected, a risk that I be reported to have seen and ignored my guest when she stood so near my unseeing eyes. But I
would that the earth split open and swallow me rather than

4. *BL,* no. 249.

that there be found in my heart a rudeness so brutal that when
a more than human beauty, wafted so to speak by some breath
of air, enters my room, I fail to acknowledge her presence (so
much at least, if more should be improper) and, where propri-
ety permits, attempt to entertain her brightly. How pitiable a
thing is enforced silence, since one who for lack of speech can
deny nothing confesses guilt on all counts. Now, because I have
no command of French (my lady speaks only her native
French), I shall be innocent in the eyes of all, but not forgiven
by the one lady in whose court my plea must stand or fall. He
who was wounded long ago by the Aemonian spear,[5] from that
same spear won help. Since your gift of charming speech (which
made me forget myself and ignore the lady) has imposed upon
me this embarrassment, your gift of charming speech ought to
relieve me of this embarrassment and restore me to my lady's
good graces.

More's Verses Punning on His Name[6]

You are foolish if you entertain any long hope of remaining
here on earth. Even a fool can advise you, More, on this score.
Stop being foolish and contemplate staying in heaven; even a
fool can advise you, More, on this score.

5. Achilles' spear, which both wounded and cured Telephus (see
Ovid, *Metamorphoses,* XII, 112, and XIII, 171–72).

6. *BL,* Appendix, no. 7: According to his early biographer, Nicholas
Harpsfield, More wrote these verses in 1532. The original Latin runs
as follows:

> Moraris si sit spes hic tibi longa morandi,
>   Hoc te vel morus, More, monere potest.
> Desine morari et coelo meditare morari,
>   Hoc te vel morus, More, monere potest.

INDEX